Falling Together

returning to the source

Imetai M. M. Henderson, D. O. M.

To the memory of

O'Sensei M. M. Nakazono

Any book is a gem. Even those that do not appeal to us may be precious to someone else. Every gem starts as a stone that must be taken from the earth and then cut and polished. Although I dug up this stone, many other hands have helped in the cutting and polishing. I want to thank the friends and patients who looked this book over at various points in the past eight years. Specifically, my deepest thanks to Abbey Mayer and Tamar Davir Schulte for their invaluable help with editing. And profound thanks to Diane Wohl, for help any and every time.

INTRODUCTION

CULTIVATING THE PRIMARY RELATIONSHIP

In well over 20 years of professional practice of traditional Oriental medicine, I have experienced small and large realizations. Some have crept up on me; others have arrived whole. Many have arrived whole after years of creeping up. This book is about one such realization.

Any new theories come from somewhere. I think we can trace them back to Spirit. Some call Spirit "God," while others call it the Creator. Still others name Spirit the Source. What we call it is unimportant. It is the communication itself that is essential.

This book is about how we have learned to separate our identities from our bodies, and thus from one another. We have all, at one time or another, neglected our primary relationship, if we are even aware it exists, which is the one our consciousness (our ego or mind) has with our bodies.

I hope this book will offer us a way to heal ourselves and, in doing so, to heal our Earth. The healthy continuation of life on this planet depends on our individual efforts to be whole. After all, it is hard to tackle a global problem individually; it seems to make more sense for each of us to tend what we can touch daily . . . our own internal wars and chaos. As we do, our ability to act effectively in the outer world increases. Otherwise, we bring our own chaos and lack of clarity into all our interactions, with predictable results.

Most of our daily activities center around trying to find or build a place where we can be okay. We try to gather enough money, prestige, power, or even food. Yet the place where we are always okay exists inside us, and we can all get there.

There is a place in both men and women that, when it has enough of our conscious attention and direction, can be filled with power. This place is different for men and women, and I call it the Source. It is a neutral place, a place of infinite wisdom that may have wants but has no needs. When we as people come from understandings other than those of the Source, we are typically in a dualistic, win-lose paradigm and are separated from ourselves and from others. To experience peace, we must return to our Sources and let our consciousness learn to flow from there.

The whole of society's ills revolves primarily around the antagonistic relationship between masculine and feminine energies. This "war of the sexes" takes place within ourselves first, and then is projected onto the larger stage of our lives. As long as we operate from places within us that have no power, or that feel powerless, we will always strive for control. The sad part about control is that without true, neutral power backing it, it eventually becomes domination. Power struggles occur only when we feel powerless.

In order to understand the terms this theory is couched in, knowledge of my background will be helpful. It may also be useful to know a little bit more about me, since any theory whose genesis is Spirit must be, by necessity, filtered through an imperfect human being. The following will allow you to understand my viewpoints and from where they have stemmed. It may also help you to understand my mistakes and misinterpretations.

My birth was not unusual for the time and place—New York City in the mid 1960s. I was born to a Jewish mother and a black father who were not together. When I was four, my mother joined the dojo (school) of a

Japanese sensei (teacher) for the study of aikido, a martial art. I studied as well, and still do. At age seventeen I began training in traditional Japanese acupuncture with the same sensei at the Kototama Institute, and after graduation, I began private practice.

I was privileged to have been raised in three diverse cultures. I was visually black, raised by a Jewish mother following Japanese culture through a sensei who was unique to most Japanese people I had met. Much of sensei's medical and martial training occurred prior to World War II, before many Japanese traditions were lost.

I grew up in parts of New Mexico, California and New York, and in many of the schools I attended, I was the only black student. Thus, as an adult, it has been obvious to me that although I fit in with no culture perfectly, I am at home in each of them. That turn of events has given me an unusual vantage point. Further, the training demanded by Eastern medicine teaches one to look at any given element through a neutral lens, for finding a root cause among a plethora of symptoms is always paramount.

One thing (among many) that I have struggled with is male chauvinism. It is inherent in many cultures and was a strong undercurrent during my youth. As a young man in my twenties, I found myself either putting women on a pedestal or using them. I was taught that men had different rules to follow in relationships—that we were innately superior and that we were to be cared for by women. More specifically, we were to use women for our care. That is one way to organize our lives, of course, but it is not effective if we wish to be in a helpful, supportive relationship with ourselves. Misogyny as a lifestyle leads to destruction of our own inner feminine energies, as well as to a derangement of how we look at women in our lives.

In a man, feminine energy can be described as the interior of the body itself. That is, everything that supports us yet is invisible to us. The feminine is the energy we as men depend on within ourselves to give us rest, peace and a sense of true power. Many men use women to feel powerful, secure and loved. Rarely do we cultivate our own inner feminine energy to grant us those things. We use another life to do it for us.

The practice and habit of using the feminine has been modeled to masculine energies for untold generations. However, if we as men dominate and use women, we are doing the same thing to our own feminine energies. Women often deplete their own energy by conducting an inner dialogue more unkind than any that would be tolerated in the outside world. Everyone has masculine and feminine energies that occupy different anatomical areas, but masculine energy typically sits in the mind for both sexes.

It was cosmic justice that my practice always consisted of at least 95 percent women. I could not, over time, continue to honor the misogynistic examples I had been exposed to. After treating dozens of women whose men had betrayed them, I began to take stock of my own betrayals of women. As the years went by, I became adept at treating women, and those treatments have evolved to reveal where women are at their most powerful and at peace. My search into my own life—and where I find my own power and peace—is my background for presenting the male viewpoint.

If I continue to organize myself around my brain or genitals, I will always be a slave to what I have been taught black men are. Or loyal to my interpretation of what Jewish men are. Or prisoner to my imagination of what Japanese men are. Only when I can learn to keep my energy in my Source can I operate from a place that is in alignment with Spirit. Spirit has no favorites. We are all favored in the realm of Spirit.

Men and women generally conceive of the world through an accumulation of life energy in certain physical areas. That amalgam translates into the perceptions of the head, the heart or the genitals, and it is through these systems that we currently organize our energies. The hopes, desires, guilt, fears and thoughts of each particular system create personas based on that organization.

The organization appears to be somewhat social: Men are expected to be mentally able, sexually dynamic, and powerful, as well as financially able. Women are expected to be either mentally capable or prone to emotional extremes, and to be sexually alluring. They are also to provide comfort and stability, and be nurturing. These seem to be the limits of our social organization.

Men who have soft hearts are denigrated, as are women who desire but do not need anyone.

Within this book the words head, mind and brain are used interchangeably, as are the terms womb and uterus. When I use the word dualistic, I mean a polarization of energy, which leads to catch-22 paradigms of good-evil, black-white, etc. The heart, for women, ought to be understood in the traditional Western way, as the seat of emotion. This is because with women, the heart's energy is expansive.

With men, where the heart's energy is receptive, the heart can be understood in the Eastern sense, as the seat of joy. With men, too, the heart holds the functions of emotion, but in a different way, which will be explained in later chapters. In some forms of Eastern medicine, the liver system actually holds emotion, and I place it with the heart system in this text.

It bears special and specific consideration that the womb and genitals are separate and distinct systems.

Our brains are trained to react with an adrenaline response to anything that might put us in physical danger. Our society has taught us to expand the mandate to include anything that challenges our egos or our emotions. To organize our energies in different ways will, naturally, result in different perceptions and experiences.

Backlash is what occurs when the brain, heart (in women) or genitals become afraid of the new balance of life energy and then appropriate all or most of the life energy for a time to assuage the feelings of losing control. As an example of backlash, one patient, after putting all her energy into her Source (her womb) during treatment, found that she could not stop thinking for two days. She could not, in her words, "get out of her head," having returned to her habitual mind-guided worldview in order to deal with the unusual experience of a new energetic organization.

The following chapters will attempt to explain how we are currently organized and how we can re-organize ourselves so that we can think, act and feel from the places the Source or Creator designed us to be guided from. The word Creator is used not in a religious sense, but in the sense of the Will of Life, the energy that heals our wounds, grows us from young to old, and takes care of the infinite details that are beyond our knowing.

All opinions and theories in this work are my own. Some insights and ideas are borrowed and some are adapted. I have tried not to take credit for a theory when the origin of the theory in question is known; however, no authors are named specifically.

All mistakes and errors in this book are also my own and should in no way reflect on my teachers, my schooling or my patients.

Further, in no way do I wish to portray myself as one who has "mastered" anything. I own to being, like all of us, a work in progress. To paraphrase one poet, "We are, none of us, done with our changes."

CHAPTER ONE

The purpose of this book is to help us reconnect with our primary relationship, the one between our consciousness (and its various parts) and our body, and further, to organize ourselves in such a way that the whole of who we are becomes available to us so that we have active, conscious choice as we interact with ourselves and with the world.

The Source is the bubbling spring in the Universe from which we all have come. It is our starting point, and the place from which we, in our totality, arise. The Source is our initial inspiration for life and, as such, houses our original blueprint for life and health. The Source is the place from which we have all experienced miracles and complete safety, even if we forget this connection.

When science finally usurped religion's mantle, true belief in magic died. Predating that, we humans moved from multiple deities to monotheism, and we lost the ability to consider the effect of more than one intelligent energy living within us. Ancient Greeks might speak of being commanded by Pallas Athena and being privy to her Divine Wisdom, or of feeling that a quaking in their soul was attributable to the bolt of Zeus. Cupid was a major force in ancient life. He had characteristics that we all have but are taught to repress. Other ancients might speak of planetary influences and would take care to honor all the gods and goddesses. Deities had parts of the body that were sacred to them, and it would just be a trick of words to call those parts organs or meridians or chakras. For several thousand years we have been moving away from the true rich relationship with ourselves that our ancient ancestors were aware of.

If we call ourselves one, and worship One, we are ignoring that we are more complex than one. Yet by considering the multitudes within ourselves, we do eventually end up back at One. We can call this the Source. The most important ongoing thing in life is to be aware of our relationship to it.

Some of my religious patients have had difficulty with the concept of the Source, thinking that it was accepting another God when, to them, there was but one true God. My understanding is that the Source is our physical connection to the Creator, whomever or whatever we believe that to be. Thus, seeking the Source creates the doorway between the human and the divine. Accepting the Source is the same as accepting the self and has nothing to do with religion. The Source has no concern or desire to control whatever the consciousness chooses to worship.

The Source is our inner body and inner life, and houses our original life seed (DNA). To seek a conscious relationship with it will revolutionize our way of being. This is because instead of looking to the external world for love, care, and logic, we will, as a point of honor and pragmatic wisdom, be able to give these things to ourselves. Thus when the external world offers us anything, we can judge it from a full, relaxed place instead of a needy, weak and survival-based viewpoint.

The Source can guide us perfectly, but it will not take energy from other systems. The Source must be given the energy of free will, or be asked to take it by the consciousness presently in charge.

This Source does not ask, does not fight and does not argue, and for these reasons it is almost completely ignored. Our society, our ideas and tendencies that form it, are based on competition. There is no healthy competition within an organism. Perhaps an argument can be made that competition between countries or companies can be healthy. Perhaps. But not within the body. Internal competition leads to dysfunction and illness, mental or physical.

When we learn to seek and find our Source, we are fine. When we are fine or at ease, our internal world is in harmony. Thus, our supportive internal relationship has created an atmosphere that can be likened to perfect weather for us, in all our complexity, to live and grow easily. Physically, we have simply moved our energy into a certain configuration within our internal systems. These systems have been simplified for this text, and will be explained later in this chapter. This specific configuration enables each system to function comfortably within the scope of its power—to be relaxed.

This material is meant to provide a method for consciously and concretely pursuing the place within where we are fine. Should we lose that sense of being fine, this book will present ways to monitor where we are so that we can address any internal disharmony and then return to our original organization, in which we are always at ease. These methods can help move our energies to the appropriate systems so that everything is functioning peacefully.

Caring for the primary relationship with our body with the intent to treat ourselves as well as we do those closest to us (or farthest, depending on who receives the best of us) develops into conscious interaction with our Source. Health deteriorates in direct relation to how far our identities are from consciously interacting with our bodies in a kind, fair and supportive way. Healing is created when the Source system is freed to act by the mind and its learned logic, and is able to balance energy in the affected areas or systems at a speed and vibration that will change depending on variables such as emotion, climatic conditions or living situations.

Every moment asks: What is required to blend with the prevailing life energy in the Universe (sometimes the prevailing life energy is manifested by a person, sometimes by a world situation, etc.)? When we blend with this energy, we live a life filled with exhilaration. When we fight it, we become ill. But we cannot blend with the forces of the world mentally until our minds grasp that life itself is a force and our integrated selves are all we have riding its huge wave. In that light, the marriage of mind to body must be a happy union in order for us to have any chance at perceiving a joyful life.

Though there are numerous definitions for it, life energy can be defined as the capacity for movement and the power that animates our body, our systems and our consciousness. It is also the same energy that moves, seen and unseen, through the universe. This definition of life energy is perhaps vague, or perhaps too all-inclusive, but most of us have a sense of what it is. To make it simpler, life energy is our awareness. It is what makes things happen, as well as the part of us that registers what occurs.

In differentiating between many states of life energy, the focus will be and must be on the level of consciousness. We will be dealing directly only with conscious perceptions. However, our conscious perceptions have a profound effect on our subconscious and unconscious life energy. All the explanations in this book are meant for our brains, so that we can better understand where we are and why it is possible and desirable to arrive somewhere else.

YIN AND YANG

In Japanese medicine, the Chinese character for yin translates to "The shady side of the mountain." The character for yang translates to "The sunny side of the mountain." Yin and yang are always relative and always changing. What is yin in the morning when the sun rises, might well be yang in the afternoon. Anything might be more yin at midnight and more yang at midday.

Yin has the characteristics of stillness, dark, cool, nurturing, weight, downward direction, slow steadiness, patience, acceptance, etc.

Yang has the characteristics of movement, light, heat, quick activity, upward direction, speed, growth, seeking change, excitement, etc.

Of course, there is no pure yang or pure yin. Everything is a mixture of both. There is a unity preceding yin and yang, as there is a wholeness, a shifting balance, once they join. This is true for every creation in the universe. Yin at its extreme becomes yang, and vice versa.

Yang is considered to be male and positive, and yin female and negative. Paradoxically, yang is often characterized as soft and diffuse, while yin is hard and brittle. With yin and yang, positive and negative are only magnetic poles. When the northern hemisphere is in summer (yang), the southern is in winter (yin). Simple balance. One hemisphere is not superior merely by position. However, as they are always in relation, it is not a static system. Each system has a yin aspect and a yang aspect. Yin is the form, and yang is the function or the activity. Taking the brain as an example: the gray matter, the cells themselves, are yin. The electrical functions, the firing of neurons, etc., are yang. Another example is the computer. The computer itself is yin, and the electricity that animates it is yang.

Yin holds the capacities of power and wisdom, while yang holds intent and will. It is important that we use our power and wisdom to direct our intent and will. If intent and will come first, we are expanding without first contracting. Thus we do not have power and wisdom anchoring our intentions and wills. We act from an unsupported place and have no power to fuel our yang aspects. It is as if we jump before crouching to gather power. Yin is meant to support, nurture, calm and direct the yang. As some Native American women say, "We walk behind our men. . . but only to tell them where to go."

Yin's intelligence is unknowable. It can be experienced, but not logically accessed. We can experience a cut on our finger, but we cannot consciously feel how the cells actually separated, and we cannot know logically how to consciously heal the cut. We can only know yang energy, as humans. This is because the known exists in a logical framework that is consistent in its repeatable nature. Women, however, through their womb, can communicate and experience yin energy even though they may never be able to logically explain it. They can sit in the place of the unknowable and can even organize their consciousness from there. It is an awesome and matchless gift. The Source in both men and women has the yin quality of receptivity. Thus men, as well, may never be able to resort to logic to explain what it is to have all their energy in their hearts, but the experience is available. It is up to each person to see if it is desirable for her or him. I can report than no one I have met who has experienced energy in his or her Source has found it less than wonderful.

A preponderance of yang energy is what we know as being awake. Yang activity feeds off of yin form. When we sleep, we contract, sink and descend into the stillness of yin energy, from where we replenish the capacity to expand. If we expand more than we contract, we become ill. If we contract more than we expand, we become ill. Men have a higher range of expanding life energy than women; women can contract their life energy to a deeper level than men.

HARD AND SOFT

Hard versus soft is largely an emotional distinction, but a critical one, and it generally fits into the qualities of yin and yang, respectively. Hard, at its extreme, includes the following qualities: autocratic, brittle, authoritative, unfeeling, domineering, territorial, explosive, emotionally unavailable (or available to the senses of anger, vengeance, retribution), blaming others, self-importance, egocentrism, rage and hate. In short, anything that inhibits anything else. The quality of egocentrism, for example, inhibits the give-and-take inherent in all fundamentally sound relationships.

Soft includes the qualities of inappropriate tenderness, self-sacrifice, emotionally undifferentiated and easily wounded, other-validated, without boundaries, self-blaming, overly sensitive (to emotions, world situations, news, etc.), unprotected, prone to depression, worry, sadness, victimhood, ennui or fear, and any qualities that allow the self to be used. (These are extreme examples for clarity's sake.) For example, the quality of inappropriate tenderness may result in a tendency to give when it is at our own expense, or to a recipient who is not appropriate, or to give at inappropriate times.

In healthier people, the qualities are mixed rather well. It is only when we become out of balance that the qualities of hard and soft become polarized.

Many of us are confused about whether we ought to identify ourselves as hard or soft. As men, many of us have been taught that men ought to be hard. Part of it is experiential. As teenagers, sensitive and soft males often experience the following: Girls like them, but give love and their bodies to males who are hard, who treat them with insensitivity. These harder males tease, ostracize and sometimes beat up the softer boys. So we as men often learn to be hard. Then, as we get older, we meet some men who are soft, and we meet some women who like softer men. Soft men are not, as a rule, respected by other, harder, men. So we develop a split. With men and with certain women, we become hard. With other women and perhaps some male friends, we become soft. Sometimes the yin and yang split becomes so extreme that we feel that we are two distinct people. We are. We have organized our perceptions and identity around two different energies. Hard people are attracted to soft people or situations, while soft people are attracted to hard energies. It is a strange phenomenon that a person can be sadistic in one relationship and masochistic in another, but it is understandable in this light. Once the energies are set, shifting them is difficult. Few people can cycle from hard to soft with freedom. Once a relationship with a person, job, or living situation is in place and agreed on either tacitly or energetically, the hard energy has to always be hard, and the soft energy always soft. In the end, in order to gain some breathing room, people often have to terminate relationships to regain some sense of neutrality.

A more effective yin-yang pair is possible when we evolve the conceptions of hard and soft into being open or closed.

Hard or soft is a static identity. Open or closed is simple and based on choice. Open your hand, then close it. When it is open, we can receive or support something. When it is closed, we can either protect something within our hand, or not take whatever is being offered. It involves a simple decision, and it is not an identity. It is not static, but fluid, and it contains the graceful aspects of life.

The Source in men and women has both qualities, open and closed. An open womb can expand its view and power to the external world, and a closed womb is simply focusing inward. A soft uterus collapses, and a hard uterus becomes stagnant.

An open, receptive heart in a man has the qualities of gentleness and joy, whereas a soft heart leads to perceiving ourselves as victim to either internal or external phenomenon. A closed heart chooses to not become emotionally involved. A hard heart needs to protect itself, so either it attacks emotionally (often preemptively), which leads to brutality, or it disconnects. If we squeeze our fist as tight as we can for five minutes, it will first hurt and then become numb. At that point we do not know what is painful and what is not. Numbness is a result of over-hardening.

We, as men, are often taught to use our genitals as weapons, to "pound," to "nail," to subdue, to conquer, to prove our power. We use our penises, the part of us that can come closest to a woman's creation energy, in the service of a hard head or heart that has defined manhood as a certain insensitivity.

Balanced men with open hearts are gentle because they know their strength and do not want to injure anything through numbness. It is our job as men to use what is naturally hard in us in a gentle way. We are bigger, in general, than women. With the power vested within our bodies comes great responsibility. As Shakespeare wrote, "O, it is excellent to have a giant's strength; but it is tyrannous to use it like a giant."

A hard heart in either gender leads to brutality, directed either within or without. A young woman I was treating was living with a man she was in love with, and every place in their house had something in it from his earlier relationships. There were inscribed books, as well as photos of him and other women on the walls. She would run across letters from his ex-lovers in the desk they shared. In both energetic and concrete senses, there was no place she could go within the house that was free of the elements of whom he had loved and slept with. When she confronted him, he said that they were important parts of his life and that if she wanted pictures of her past relations on the wall, that was fine with him. She said that whenever she talked with him, she felt foolish for even bringing it up.

After many years of treating patients, I have come to conclude that on this topic, regardless of the psychological reasons behind it, some people are jealous of their partner's past relationships, and some are not.

When we checked in with her Source, she said that she was a jealous woman, without any negative self-judgment whatsoever. She wanted to be the only one her lover saw and wanted and did not want to be reminded of the times when his heart had been with other women.

Her heart and mind had entered into battle. When her heart had more energy, and she identified herself from that place, in its softness toward her partner, her heart would tell her that she ought to be "cool" with his past and its display. That if she loved him, she would always have to act cool about what he did, had done or wanted. The fact was, she was not fine with it, but her heart had decided that she just had to take it. After all, she was free to do the same if she wanted to. She wanted peace in their home, but could not get it with her heart taking the stance that certain things ought to be okay with her.

When her mind had the most energy, she would become hard after seeing something upsetting. She would get angry at the constant reminders of his romantic past, convinced that he was insensitive and mean to put her in that position. She would then, with her mind firmly in control, try to hurt him for disrespecting her. If she did not let herself fight with him, she would simply attack herself. Hard energies seem to say, "I am going to make someone pay for something, whether I imagined it or not." The result was a young, talented woman with almost no energy. It was all being used up by her identity pinging back and forth in the conflict between her two systems, one soft and one hard. Whenever she won on one side, she lost on the other. Since it was all her own energy, in the end she always lost. I find this a beautiful example of most conflict in our world.

In her case, it was a matter of getting the hard and soft both to learn the options of becoming open and closed—to get them out of a static position. The heart had to accept that no matter her love for him, it was showing no self-love to ignore the facts: it did not bother him, but it did bother her. Self-love dictated that she make sure that she could move around her home without a constant bracing. In learning to close her heart (somewhat) to him, she was able to see what it was like to open to her own preferences first. Her Source's solution was that she ask him to keep one room in their home for himself and confine all reminders of his past relationships in that space. She could then insure that she was not energetically shocked merely by going home. If she chose to go into his private room, she would know what to expect.

In treatment we brought to consciousness the fact that when her brain went hard, it was defending what her truth was, but only by its own definition. With the mind, we focused on learning to open its energy. The logic he used was true for him: her past did not bother him. By opening to the view that his being true to himself had nothing to do with her, she was able to see that her own truth would logically have very little to do with him. She framed a paradigm that worked for her. Her Source's logic decided that if anything bothered her in her home, she should not have to see it. She added that in fairness, he should have a place for what he wanted to keep from his past. After a little while she was able to look at the anger that would come up either against herself or against him as a simple indication that she was feeling victimized. If she felt that way, her survival system, the mind, would attack the attacker, whether it was him or her own heart. With this understanding, she experienced herself as having an effective choice. By choosing to open to something or close to it, she could take care of herself more easily. That choice allowed both systems to work with the definitive statement that the Source had made. Once she accepted that she was jealous, she was able to work with that, not only with what she thought he wanted or how she wished she was. It allowed her to enhance her life and relationship, rather than merely surviving it.

THE TRIPLE HEATER

The Triple Heater (cf. Triple Warmer or Triple Burner) is used to represent the three levels of our body in traditional Oriental medicine. Like yin and yang, it is relative. We can use this model to help us determine where our life energy is, and then how much of it is there. Traditionally, the three Heaters are divided anatomically as above the diaphragm, between the diaphragm and navel, and below the navel. In this text the Upper Heat is located above the clavicles (the neck and up), the Middle Heat between the clavicles and diaphragm, and the Lower Heat below the diaphragm.

Let us look first at the upper heat, which contains the consciousness and the mind. Personalities organized here place the most emphasis on what can be predicted, what is known, and what can be expected based on that criteria. The basic organization in the brain is logic, though it is often the logic of a child, pure cause and effect. Regardless of what is being perceived, the mind leaps to a historic cause and renders a course of action. Our brains operate on a logic that says I must do A, or B will happen. This survival tactic may have been critical to us when we were younger, but we are in a different world as adults, with a myriad of options. However, these options are useless as long as we continually force events into the same context, which we have become adept at doing through ceaseless repetition.

Some of us, as children, in order to insure our own survival, had to insure that our caretakers could take care of us. Thus we developed many tactics to make ourselves safe. If it meant that we had to look after our parents so that we, in turn, would be taken care of, we did so. As adults, we no longer need the same care we did as children. We can feed, clothe and shelter ourselves.

However, our brains still operate on the survival tactics we developed as children. Logic based on those childhood needs robs us of adult options and experience. Our brains usually claim the emotions of anxiety, fear, stress and obsession in order to justify the need for so much life energy. The brain can project either internally or externally and has been known to debate or attack itself.

Whenever we castigate ourselves or think about options not in the moment, we are in our brains. The mind may also, under the guise of protecting the heart from being injured, keep energy from the heart. Conversely, the brain may choose to interpret events in ways that hurt the heart's emotions, so that it can then justify calling in more energy to "solve" or protect itself or the heart from similar events happening again. The events do happen again, whenever the heart gets too involved—i.e., takes too much life energy from the brain—or even when the brain gets bored.

Typically, upper heat people keep 60 to 90 percent of their conscious life energy above their necks. Energy creates pressure, and pressure in a brain surrounded by bone often leads to symptoms. Of course, many people have benign relationships with their brains, but even friendly relationships with the mind can still cause too much energy to be focused there. It is my experience that a brain needs two to four percent of conscious life energy to function most effectively.

The middle heat contains the heart. Imbalanced personalities organized here identify themselves by what they feel emotionally. They are directed more by feeling and intuition than by logic. They use worry, feelings of duty, rumination, jealousy, anger, depression and frustration to draw more life energy into their heater. There is often a battle here between the logic of the brain and the comfort of the emotions. The more energy we put into our emotional system, the more we will feel, and because of the war with the brain, what we feel is often translated or interpreted as negative. Unfortunately, whenever we have emotions that move away from joy, symptoms develop. Habitual emotions that include joy strengthen us; those without joy weaken us.

Middle heat people usually have between 40 and 60 percent of life energy within the system. In women, again, two to four percent is all that is necessary.

Conversely, men ought to focus as much life energy within the thorax as possible and then open the chest by visualizing the ribs retracting like a car antenna or falling open; anything that opens the rib cage. We do not need to focus specifically on the heart organ; gathering energy into our chests around our hearts is optimal. Putting 100 percent life energy into the heart and keeping the chest closed can lead to feelings of pressure and being clogged. By focusing the energy and then causing our heart energy to open, we can access feelings of fullness, joy, love, happiness and fearlessness.

The lower heat is a little trickier to explain as it contains the subconscious. And, as mentioned earlier, it is necessary to differentiate between the womb or prostate and the genitals. A woman can benefit from directing as much energy as possible to her womb. Putting too much energy in the genitals results in the development of a persona driven by the heart or brain. When the mind becomes involved, it will interpret the energy in the genitals in the ways in which the person has been taught (by parents, society, religion, etc.) to look at sexuality. Those teachings are almost invariably limiting and, especially for women, negatively judgmental. For men, the teachings tacitly or otherwise communicated to us are usually about controlling, dominating or using.

When the heart involves itself with genital energy, we have a situation where emotion becomes the arbiter for sensuality or sexuality. For a man whose heart is not full, genital energy becomes a symptom of need. A hard-hearted person uses partners as tools for feeling powerful; a soft-hearted person lets his sexual and intimate energy be at another's whim. For a full-hearted man, genital energy comes down from the heart and enlivens the genitals.

Women's emotional capacity, when confused with sexuality, can drain a woman because she will be acting from an incomplete persona. Her heart energy, unlike a man's, is not the system designed to determine if sex is good for all the heaters. Once a woman focuses on her Source, her mind and heart (emotion) root and entwine around a larger, more inclusive truth of who she is. Womb energy, when full, grounds a woman completely and lets her feel what is right for any system. The Source is the home of creation energy. Thus it is vitally important that whatever comes in contact with it, especially physically, be its choice.

An energy-filled womb is a woman's Source and allows a woman peace, joy, time and clear differentiation between each and every system and desire. It does not feel any stress, fear or need. When the energy is pooled within the womb, the Source can decide how much energy each of the other systems needs within each moment.

The trick of the lower heat is that it is also the home of the unknowable. Mystery lives here, and it can only be experienced, not explained or understood through language. This is the center that relates most intimately with the body and sensation.

In men, putting too much life energy, either hard or soft, into the prostate and genitals over a lifetime leads to a high probability of compromised prostates and soft genitals. After all, years spent focusing on hardness are bound to lead to the other extreme (yang, at its extreme, becomes yin). When we focus to an extreme on yang energy, we deplete our ability to contract, and then our energy becomes yin (stillness and non-motion), as it is all that remains. It is ironic to see men's focus so genitally directed and centered.

Balanced men are far less interested in sexual activity for any reason other than connection. When the heart is full, the genitals serve that strength and thus open. It is only with hard hearts and hard genitals that we further this societal sickness of numb sex. In general we men are conscious of only a small amount of what is happening during a sexual experience. If we can feel or receive only a tiny bit of life energy through sex, and life energy is what makes us feel more alive, then we always yearn for more. We stalk it, hunt it, and ultimately, kill it. However, if we learn to fill our heart energy, we are, by definition, full. We can have sex or not, without needing or yearning for it or confusing it with being alive.

We each have our own emptiness. We each have something that we identify as critical to our happiness in the outside world. That substance is a macrocosmic example of our microscopic lack. For example, if we see money, career, community, recognition, love, or sex as something we lack, there is a corresponding lack energetically inside of us, an internal organization that creates that lack. When we fill our place of power inside, the external lack will no longer exist. This does not mean that when we have our energies in order, we will instantly hit the lottery and the money outside will match the energy inside (though who knows?). Rather, in reorganizing our internal energetic structure, the perception and reality of what is externally important changes.

Our personalities, formed by the distribution of energy in our bodies, creates our perception of reality and our memory of experience. We all have several personae. Too much energy—which can be emphasis, worry, guilt, obsession, etc.—focused in places not designed to function with that much pressure creates additional personae from those places. We have many hells within us, and one heaven. Hell is merely being who we are not—or, not being all of who we are.

Only one system in a man and one in a woman is perfectly capable of guiding and healing all other systems. Of course, it is the one we have been trained for millennia to ignore, abjure, and avoid. The peace that flows from having everything following the natural order is matchless. Most of us have glimpsed it. There are many external activities that can, even if just for an instant, remind us of what it is to be whole. This book is about doing it within ourselves and living in it constantly, so that we never again need to be dependent on anything outside of ourselves for our own bliss. We can enjoy the external, sure, but we will not need it. We have options.

CHAPTER TWO

THE BRAIN

From the tenor of my writing up to now, you may have gotten the feeling that the brain is the enemy. This is not so, although it is often necessary to remind ourselves of that fact. The mind is a system that has been taught that it is responsible for our survival. Usually the brain will be honestly shocked that it is not the ruler or the Source of our lives. After all, any conscious circulation of life energy is taught or, at least, learned.

Many of the rewards, the "strokes," that society offers come to us when we have the opportunity or the drive to hone our brains well enough to take a position in society as a teacher, doctor, lawyer, accountant, nurse, teacher, captain of industry, etc. However, let us be clear: one aspect of these professions is simply having the great good fortune to be in a position where one can put to use the capacity we all have for memorizing certain facts and mastering certain rules (and paying the requisite dues).

A proficiency at manipulating data does not by default make the mind the place designed by an incredibly multilayered life to apprehend criteria other than logic. Life does offer logic, but there are realms of other experiences (love, parenthood, duty, global stress, religious loyalties, etc.) that function within their own logic, (i.e., they are not necessarily repeatable). Anyone who has ever participated in a relationship knows that emotional logic runs in a way particular to each individual and does not always reach the same conclusions.) Our minds are not designed to understand those mischievous elements, but life does give us a system that is conscious of its (and thus, our) connection to all life. This system can take what is offered and make a relaxed, logical (to all systems) and confident decision based on joy instead of survival.

The key to growth is the inclusion of that which already is. With this in mind, the Source takes our continued survival as a given pre-condition of any decision.

The brain thinks it rules: if we truly examine what a developed memory for "facts" will bring us in our present world, the benefits offered in socioeconomic terms are irrefutable, as is the fact that money rules decision making in a majority of cases. As the system that "brings home the bacon," it is certainly understandable that brains believe they are the rulers of our lives. But given the fact that most of us sharing this mind-centered paradigm are suffering either somatically or emotionally, it is at least worthy to consider that there is an internal location that is concerned with joyful participation by all dimensions of our lives, all our parts and personae.

If we can develop relationships with other people, nations, pets, TV shows, brands of phones or computers, is it so far-fetched to consider a relationship with the part of that self that is silent—but whose love for us can be witnessed in the very fact that we are, this second, alive? Is it naïve or insane to consider that what happens within our skin is at least as conscious, complex and desirous of peace as is the consciousness concerned with what happens outside our skin?

In Eastern medicine, each system or function has a Ki (cf. Chi, Qi), an energy that is fundamentally a vibration with intent, that is, an energy that precedes form yet still has a speed, density, direction and purpose. There is Protective Ki, Nutritive Ki, Primal Ki, etc. Different Ki have their own intelligence, which is communicative and aware, but that awareness is located somewhere other that in our waking consciousness—in our Sources. Being aware of this allows us the potential to actually communicate with our own Ki, if we can find our Sources. These different Ki are aware of, among other things, realms such as dreams, digestion, emotions, the immune system, and if the weather outside requires our pores to open or close.

The Ki are aware of the persona we consider our identity, even as we remain oblivious to the very mechanics of energy and power and divine love that keep each cell acting with cohesion and loyal duty toward our whole being. And since these Ki are conscious and meet at our Source, we have a true inner council that wants a conscious relationship with who we think we are, wherever that is, whenever or however it happens.

The Source is the silent guardian that sits at the center of our being and witnesses our whole lives. And because it loves us, it trusts and believes in us and gives us what guidance it can. But our taught limitations allow the Source to act only in tiny ways, if at all. In order to not shock the consciousness, the Source stays silent, and over the years our link to our Source becomes overgrown and the path to it forgotten.

True power is generally gentle, and vast power can be almost unnoticeable except for its effects. As we age, what is truly gentle, easy and vast internally seems to be slowly forgotten. Our Source will rarely directly act, and even when it does, we cannot perceive it as a distinct force, for the simple reason that we have not been taught that it exists within us, and it is so vast that it encompasses our mind and every other system.

We might ask, Why doesn't the true ruler, the Source, simply take power? Because it does not stir unless requested. True power does not want or need what it already is. The Source supports everything but acts only if asked to by the consciousness, which includes our intent and will. The Source assumes that if we don't ask it to guide us, we want to guide ourselves. Yet we never were given the option of guiding ourselves back to our own Sources. So our Source watches, even if we choose paths through brambles or fire.

Our Source is ruthless in protecting its boundaries, even between it and our conscious selves. If our Sources treat us with the exquisite respect of giving us free choice, why not choose to find a way to bring our minds closer to such a safe, trustworthy energy—closer to our very cores? Few could argue that would be an unsafe place. Unknown, certainly, but also absolutely safe. The only unsafe things internally are the fallacious premises the mind has been taught to believe about ourselves and the unknown. From our Source, the place from which we have healed from or survived every wound, we can be sure of a most generous welcome.

It is from our Sources, and the Ki of Wisdom that roams there, that we can begin to reexamine what we've been taught, as well as the acts and outcomes of those teachings, and see if they are logical to the greater sense of who we are as human beings. With the Source as a mirror, we can begin to see if our current lives look anything like what would authentically make us proud to live.

A friend once told me that whenever he had to decide on an action, he simply asked himself, "Will it be easy to look at myself in the mirror tomorrow morning?" Without knowing it, he had set his relationship with an indefinable part of himself as primary to his happiness in life. To take it a step further, we can ask ourselves, "What action would make me smile with pride in the morning?"

The initial answer to the second question is an excellent doorway into where we are. If our answer involved showing someone something, then the brain took the energy. If the answer was in the vein of revealing emotion, then it has to do with the heart, and if it was sexual, it was genital. If the answer compassionately brings us to our own integrity, along with the knowledge that true power is deft and leaves the encounter (and those it encounters) with scarcely a ruffle to all concerned, it is the Source's answer.

All that to say that few are the brains that know there even is a Source, far less that they are not it. Our minds, after all, have a system of survival that has worked. If the brain's survival system works poorly, we have the stress inherent in a system trying to make something work that does not. If it works more effectively, we have a large ego because our survival system feels it is on top of matters.

In my experience, survival techniques are usually developed and in place by the time we are eight years old. Thus to a greater or lesser extent, the survival system is juvenile. It does not take into account that we are now grown, and have far more energy and capacities than we did as children.

The brain and its functions become increasingly active as we grow. It perceives our situations and devises strategies to deal with whatever seems to threaten our survival. One female patient, a 30 year old former model, had as a child a grandmother who hit her if she did not do something perfectly. The survival tactic her brain adopted was to attempt perfection at every opportunity. She was underweight, did not defecate often, and was constantly on the lookout for whatever would be construed by her family as approaching perfection. She had no sense that there was anything wrong with always pursuing an external model of perfection. The rub was that this paradigm did not give her peace, relaxation or health. Our work together involved showing her mind—that is, her ingrained definitions of her world—a broader idea of what might be acceptable.

The brain, or what we identify as the consciousness in charge, can be told gently (because many of its views and the energies that form them are no older than eight years of age) that we don't blame it, but we ought to have the option of changing our definitions. After all, why be loyal to something that does not make our lives, or our children's lives, more beautiful?

A thing to keep in mind is that the loudest, most habitual inner dialogues (as well as their content) were formed at the youngest ages. When we are young we are more whole; decisions made then have much more power because almost all our energies were focused there. As we age, we become more disparate, more dispersed. Our strategies become more focused on specific themes, like work, romance, friendships, family, and societal and religious loyalties.

This is in counterpoint to the experience some have had in childhood: the concern of actually staying alive and cared for. So as adults, the energies we invest in things are weaker, for they are on several fronts. As children, the defenses we develop are designed for the survival of the whole of who we are. Counterintuitively, the survival process demands that we cast off, disown, or hide certain aspects of ourselves. These aspects go into shadow. So, in a childhood attempt to maintain our lives, we lose parts of them. Our journey to healing demands rounding up the hidden or disowned parts and regenerating those that were cut off.

At this point I would like to introduce the idea of layers. As I understand life, everything is built, layer upon layer, from the central DNA, which is also layered. We who live today and read this are merely the surface layer of life built upon an unknowable past.

I have found in my practice that our bodies have layers too. In Eastern medicine, we often speak of an imbalance being like an onion. We have to peel off the layers until we arrive at the original wound or disease. Each layer could represent a day, month or year. Some layers are damaged over time and have to be healed over time. Other layers were damaged with single or repeated traumas. The layers are a physical and energetic book of our lives. Everything that has ever impacted us emotionally or physically, whether or not we are conscious of it, is written in our layers. That is why we need a neutral, powerful place from which to read the book which we are and then go back and reedit ourselves until the layers are free from the bubbles of trauma.

How different it would be to look over our lives with our Sources as guide, since they have witnessed everything we have ever done or felt. That, to my understanding, is true omniscience. And we have it inside. All we have ever lacked is a map to lead us back to our deepest selves.

In treating people with the intention of returning their consciousnesses to the Source, I have often seen young layers surface like bubbles. When the bubble of a younger layer surfaces, as far as our consciousness knows, we are emotionally that age and to some extent are reliving that age. So while we might be 40 or 60 years old, when certain conditions arise, so does the age when we were wounded.

When we have knowledge of our Source, we also have a place to seat our consciousness that is capable of parenting that lost or damaged layer.

An aspect of our brains' survival patterns is self-protection at all costs. Like rings on a tree, each age leaves an energetic and cellular layer within us. And through them all run our survival tactics. We cannot attack a survival strategy formed when we were young without attacking the younger selves that still exist inside us. If we successfully attack and defeat a younger aspect of ourselves, it is like undermining a building. Everything we built on top of that survival edifice will fall. The strategy must be absorbed by a more complete, more mature understanding. Once we "parent" this age within ourselves and take over the protection that was so critical then, we can start to integrate that stuck, younger self with the rest of our energies and allow it to grow up.

It is often hard to treat those nasty voices or physical habits of ours with patience, love and understanding unless we understand that they are very young. What we can compassionately care for in a child is hard to attend to if we believe it to be adult. The very strength of the habit, pattern or resistance indicates its age. The stronger it is, the younger it is. Just as we must protect our children from attacks by adults, we must protect our survival strategies from attacks by our present-day selves. We must simply offer something that works better, and that takes the survival strategy to a new level, if it is still needed. We must soothe that inner layer. Like the layers of our earth, each age we have passed maintains a physical layer in our bodies. We can reach many through various therapies, but certain layers cannot be balanced until we address the survival patterns we developed in our brains, and that must often be done verbally, with a certain logic and a most marked kindness.

Just about any mental or emotional condition can manifest physically. Even imbalances in brain chemistry often have their genesis in our youth. Sometimes a predisposition exists because our parents gave us incomplete energies at conception. This is what causes congenital conditions. Regardless of our present state, we must be able to address all parts and ages of ourselves without fear or violence.

We are all beings that contain a multitude of experiences. Those that evoked survival strategies are still stored within us, and they cannot be released unless we are prepared to face them at our present age. If we attack a survival strategy, we only trigger it and cause it to become more entrenched. If we defeat it, we invite collapse because it is also us. It can be faced and reassessed, and what is still useful can be integrated in a new, gentler way.

The brain's defenses are neural paths we have used constantly and are wired in. The mind will use the same strategy again and again, even if it does not work. To think that we must guard against so many threats, when we are generally, as humans, safer now than at any time in recorded history, is a moot point. We are not trying to convince the brain to stop protecting us. We must merely redefine what exactly we need protection from. That definition will change depending on our internal organization. Who we believe ourselves to be and what is required for our survival will vary greatly depending on whether we come from a full, curious, receptive place or from a depleted, scared and overwhelmed place.

The mind has been taught that it is the Source. Descartes' best-known observation, "I think, therefore I am," is often misinterpreted to bring even more energy to the brain. This misinterpretation is a disservice to all involved because, of course, the mind is not responsible for what it was taught. We are not even taught to question what we are taught. The brain has the willingness to try and rule because it usually loves us. But it really takes the job on because everyone models a mind-ruling paradigm, and the mind has seen nothing else reliable to emulate. The mind is the home of fear and anxiety, and it stresses and obsesses over how to alleviate those feelings. The brain must continue to ensure our survival until it understands without question that the job is not its own, that another system is designed to do it and can do it far more effectively.

In Eastern medicine, each system has certain characteristics when it is balanced and a propensity to certain symptoms when it is not. When balanced, the characteristics are known as Virtues. The kidney system rules the brain, bone and bone marrow and its virtue is wisdom and peace. When it has lost balance, the kidney system, the mind, dwells within the emotions of fear, anxiety, stress and obsession. Many are the people who revolve in those four emotional states. Virtue in any system is simply a function of the life energy being where it was designed to be, in the appropriate proportions.

Our society has trained our brains to pull far too much energy from our other systems. Each system is designed to function perfectly with relatively little, as long as it can have more energy if needed. When our brains are trained to hold more energy, they will believe there is more to do. They pull at a problem from infinite sides, turn over old experiences and memories, try to figure things out. Our brains project into the future to get something done or to avoid something else. The mind cannot figure anything out that is living. It can only play with dead information and projections into the future. It is often strained and stressed by its own functioning. Hormonal imbalances, mental imbalances and social imbalances can all trace their genesis to brains with too much energy. This also leads to the inevitable outcome of other systems having to go without adequate energy. Add to that the fact that the brain is dealing with the survival logic of an eight-year-old at best, and a baby in utero at worst, and you have got a terrified juvenile despot who takes and holds all the cards because it thinks it is trying to save the world (us).

I once made a house-call to see a woman who had been sent home from the hospital, where they said they could not do anything else for her. She had a severe eating disorder; at five feet six inches tall, she weighed just under a hundred pounds. The problem turned out to be that her mind kept telling her that what she had eaten should be enough, and it told her that after she had eaten very little. We began a series of discussions with her mind. She improved when we got her mind to admit that it had no experience in actually being a body, and that yes, it was logical that a body might need more nutrition in the winter. She even got her brain to agree that it was logical that a healing body might need richer food. Finally, as treatments made her body stronger, the brain's input was no longer pertinent. The striking thing about her condition was the disdain her mind had for her body, and the resentment her body had for her mind.

It is no surprise that many people's relationship difficulties so resemble the relationship the mind has with the body. In most relationships, be they love, work or friendship, someone usually goes for the logical, "I'll fix it" approach, while the other takes the "I feel" side of the usual balance. We can be the fixer in one relationship and the feeler in another, but we usually are static in our role within each relationship. All healing, in a broad sense, means many more options to every potentially unbalancing situation. We need to be able to be the fixer or the feeler as the moment dictates.

The mind in some people is a friendly companion. It is soft and humorous and gets embarrassed at mistakes instead of feeling shame. Those people are fortunate to have never had to live with a really nasty mind. People who have, know the feeling well. The mind can usurp all the body's energy if it wants to, feels like it needs to, gets scared, gets into a new situation—anytime. Sometimes, when we are in love, there is so much energy in the heart system that the brain is relegated to second place. Usually, however, the endorphins are so heady that the brain does not object. When we are heartbroken, however, the mind will take the energy to replay why we have been wronged. If the energy is kept in the heart, for men, and the womb, for women, the healing of a broken heart is remarkably deep and swift. Pulling energy up to the brain, replaying hurts, believing the story the mind makes up for us to perceive—all reawaken the wounding and draw out the healing process, if it ever takes place.

The mind can grow to be a tyrant. It can learn to feed off of our energy and our misery. It learns to use other systems within us as batteries (and sometimes, things outside of us. See Chapter 5). Our upset life energy creates "food" or energy for our minds. As we shift the seat of our consciousnesses to our Sources, we are immune to this kind of self-cannibalism. We will not be abused by anything, because we will interact with both the inner and outer world from a position of power and satisfaction.

The Source exists only in the present time. It can use the brain to handle details, but it is ultimately depleting for the mind to use the heart or womb, in men and women respectively, to handle its ideas, which exist outside of present time.

The Source is the only system that operates in this moment. The brain and expansive heart operate in the past or future and often use the body to mirror their projections. For example, if the brain thinks about a stressful situation in the past or future, the body reacts with adrenaline now.

To be with our Source means that this moment is paramount. The future may need to be planned for, and the Source can use the mind to do so, but if the brain plans things by itself, the plans are often based on projections about what would make us have more control in order to feel less anxiety. Our brains will scour our pasts to find what worked before and what did not, and then will set up possible futures where we either succeed or fail. We fund those internal gyrations with our life energy without ever actually being in present time. When we can actually perceive this moment from the perception of our Source, all stress and worry vanish. It is a huge gift and power to simply not be concerned about things that are outside of our fields.

All healing takes place in the present moment. Starting a regime that is in any way outside of the moment will dissipate our energies. If we let our brains decide that we will jog every day, for example, we put our bodies in the power of a system that can doggedly compel us but cannot treat us with flexibility.

To let our Source heal us now can be instantaneous. In sessions with patients, more than 90 percent of headache cases are cured after simply dropping energy from the head into the Source. Of course, as soon as the brain takes the energy back, many symptoms return. Being in our Source means being in the moment, and vice versa. Putting energy into the Source can result in total relief of symptoms; keeping it in the Source initially is a lot harder.

The more we extend ourselves into a field of time other than the present moment, the more we attenuate our life energy. This leads to increased stress, worry and more permutations about how to cope with those feelings. It is all self-created. Our brains often create reasons we might need to consult them. Our Source is there when we ask and otherwise is simply communing with the present. If we avoid the present, we avoid the only place where we have power.

Why would the brain let go of energy? How, if it has all this energy, all this power, could it ever be induced give it up? As I have said, most minds are surprised to learn that there is a Source. The consciousness genuinely thought that it was all there was to existence, and the body was just transportation, representation and recreation. Sometimes showing to the mind that there is a Source is enough for the shift. For some of us, all we need is conscious knowledge that there is a Source and where it is to be found. For some overworked brains, asking them to try letting go of some energy, just for a while, works. Usually these minds are so relieved when they can rest for a while that there is little more convincing necessary. For still others, it is a matter of asking the brain if it is ever truly peaceful. After all, filling in for the Source when you do not have the Source's capacities can be exhausting. Many brains are tired of trying to keep everything sane, and are depleted from having to function at such a high speed. Still, as it has always been the mind's job to keep us from getting tricked, the brain must be convinced with logic. And as the energy the brain is being asked to let go of does not leave the body, but is only redirected, it often assuages panic and distrust. Even if the brain can see the logic in putting energy where it is designed to be, it still may balk or lie. It helps to remind the mind that it can pull the energy back up at any time. Some brains do not believe that: they see lies in most things that create change. With brains like these, there is often a long period of conversation until the mind feels it is safe. The truth is that our brains will never know peace and never experience rest until they are in a proper relationship with the Source. The mind has wisdom when it is led by the Source, and we experience that as peace and the ability to relax. When led by anything else, we go into fear, anxiety, stress and obsession.

This is not to say that minds cannot function extremely well. Some of us may be people whose brains are highly developed. However, the questions remain: Do we have many options? Can we feel with equal facility? Is being in the moment an option? Are we able to open and close with equal facility? Do we know what peace is within our bodies? Are we self-validating, as opposed to being other-validated?[1]

---

[1] Other-validated means that our sense of who we are is dependant on external validation, be it from a person, a job or experiences. If our sense of self changes depending on whether our lover is available, if we are liked, if we get a promotion, or if we make X dollars per year, we are other-validated. Self-validation occurs when we have the final say in who we are.

If the answer to any of those questions is no, then we have a split in our life energy. Some energy is going to the options we know, and some is being used to protect against options we fear.

A common theory among New Age thinkers is that belief creates experience. A more widespread tenet in today's society is just the opposite, that experience creates belief. In shifting our viewpoints, persona and emphasis to the Source, either theory is rendered unimportant. In clinical situations, in investigating the experiences of patients, the patients and I have hit upon completely different interpretations of experience. Invariably the Source's interpretation causes a core shift in the belief about the experience. If we believe something, we interpret the happenings around us in such a way as to experience that belief. Whatever we believe or experience, it will change when we allow our energy to flow to our Source. The difference between the brain and the Source is so vast that it cannot be overstated.

One patient came in with unresolved issues, having been raped in college. She felt that the fear and trauma were still stored in her body. Memories of it had tortured her for years. Tears filled her eyes at the very thought, and she felt as though she would never recover. She understandably had difficulty in trusting men and had trouble feeling safe in her own skin. During her first treatment, in which she was guided to redirect her energy into her womb, the question arose of how her Source had experienced the rape. She said, giving voice to her Source, that it had been good. Shocked, I asked how it had been good. She said it had been very hard, but she had survived it and that had made her feel like a warrior. Her Source was proud that she had gone on after the rape with her sanity and determination to live intact. From her revised viewpoint, the rape still was not a good thing—after all, it never could be—but she had come into contact with an aspect of herself that had become stronger and more self-loving because of it. Weeks later, when I asked her about the incident, she grinned and said that she did not think about it anymore.

The focus on or avoidance of past—usually uncomfortable—experiences, and the steady fear of the future repeating those experiences, is basically why having the brain in charge is so depleting. We do not have, in general, holistic beliefs. Our beliefs are fragmented and full of win-lose clauses. When our brains win, our bodies lose. If a desire for control or pity wins, what loses? Whenever there is a winner there is, of course, a loser. Games like these, which we play with our own life energy, do have a winner. It is we who win, but it is also we, and the sacred relationship we have with ourselves, who lose. Only when the Source guides us does the paradigm shift. After all, the Source will not fight. It says either yes or no. And when it says no, we cannot argue with it, debate it or subvert it. Since it wants nothing, it needs nothing. Its food is only its connection with the divine and our own happiness. If we flee from our Source, which is our inner joy, it will let us know—sometimes with voice, sometimes through symptoms, dreams, accidents or feelings. But it will not take us over, as our brains often do. It will not demand, so it can easily be ignored and denied. However, when our dualistic mind-set becomes so fixed and unilateral that we will never release it, our Source knows. And then we die. That is the ultimate freedom the Source has: the option to no longer live.

The Source deciding that our life is over is a sad moment for a far greater reason than death. Our Source has seen that we (our consciousness) have no desire to relate to it. Our Source eventually gives up on ever being in a loving, conscious relationship with us and quietly releases its cohesion and loyalty to us. Even in choosing death, the Source is lovingly giving us what we have tacitly demanded. It is as if you have loved someone with every cell in your body and soul, and they abuse you, neglect you, use you and judge you. At some point, even our own Source despairs of us ever finding it or seeing it as a loving equal. What can a loving Life Will do at that point, except quietly pass away? The fact that most of us live for years without recalling and then honoring our deepest relationship, shows us some of the vast, unconditional love and patience our Source offers.

A brain serving the Source is free to rest in its wisdom, to channel inspiration, to deal with things as they come up, and to be free of the responsibilities it is not designed to handle. A peaceful mind that can be of service is far different from one that is stressed and demanding service.

The heart is often celebrated and consulted because it can feel any emotion. But certain emotions can injure the heart. Only two things replenish heart energy: sleep and laughter. Of course, there are medications, herbs and such for strengthening the heart muscle, but only joy heals heart energy. A man's Source is the heart, and it must be kept full and be able to close or open. Anything that gives internal joy grants men the capacity to feel through their hearts. If the heart is guided through the beliefs of the brain, then it is the brain's story made manifest through the heart's emotions. It is a hard life indeed when that happens.

Sentiment stemming from an energetically sated heart is the way to experience life as fully as we can. A friend told me that he had been to an island in Greece where there is almost no heart disease. When you go into the town, the men will put an arm around you, sit you down and ask you how you are, waiting for your answer. They laugh and cry and care. Say that to most men and they will say it is "gay." The only time many Western men are sweet with each other easily is around the possibility of violence, be it sports, war or martial arts. If you are tough enough, it seems, you can be sensitive. I have a little boy, and I was a little boy. I can see and remember how sensitive boys are. A certain tone of voice could make me cry. I said something once, unthinking, to my own son when he was quite young, and he burst into tears. As he was comforted, I recalled that I had also been like that. And so are many boys I see today, before one or both parents decide they need to be toughened up. I learned that men do not cry, and as I followed those teachings, I lost my connection to my heart. I watch my son and revel in his joy. It makes sense to me that if I teach him or allow others to teach him to harden his heart, I will be participating in hiding his capacity for joy. The search for most men involves stripping away the hardness that we have built up like a callus.

Then there are men who have denied hardness for the other extreme. They are soft and sensitive, but without knowledge or experience of the power that a man has merely because he is a man. Those two experiences are the reason why opening and closing are more effective options. We all, as men, have times to close, to become fierce and protective. And we all have times to open, let our guard down, and experience and receive joy. The reality that many of us have given up joy to experience only fierceness and hardness is very sad. It is also sad to never allow the experience of fierce protectiveness. It is amazing to feel the power that flows through our bodies as men when faced with some possible threat to us or to our loved ones. However, to experience that all the time is deadening and exhausting. Hearts, by nature, are joyful and sweet. Hearts are kind and fearless. Seeking these four qualities helps men to fill and open their hearts. When a man is in his heart, open and receptive, he is in contact with the creative elements in the universe. He is with God, whatever that is to him, and he is within a happy, loving peace.

Women, of course, have a close relationship with the heart. They have the option of, through the womb, opening or closing their emotional energy, or not engaging it at all. Women are more powerful energetically than men only when sentiment is an option, not a necessity. When Source-centered, women can be ruthless in the following sense: They can chose not to care about emotions or thoughts or anything that will compromise their lives or, if they have them, the lives of their children. Caring is simply a neutral choice. Things are yes or no, in a field of such clarity that it can seem insensitive. It is not insensitive, it is unsensitive. That is, it has no relation to sentiment at all. It is of a different order entirely. That ruthlessness is what decides how to build a body from one cell into trillions, each a hologram of the others. It is not at all mean, but it is self-serving in the greatest sense of the words. When dealing from the brain or heart without consulting her Source, a woman is stuck in the habit of serving her ego.

The womb can and does decide what to open up to with emotion and what not to. When opening the heart ceases to be an ego-based, sentimental exercise for a woman, she is free. Whatever we are ordered to do is not freedom. A balanced woman's brain is in service to her Source. That is, it will not engage in projects unless the Source feels it necessary. The phrase Sources use most often in respect to the external world is "I do not care." It is not that they have no cares, it is rather that the womb cares about the woman and her children only. The Source is involved with other things, of course, and those things may even be intensely meaningful, but it is unsensitive about them.

When several women patients were asked what their Sources felt about their mates, in essence they all said that their men were sweet and that they really, really liked them. From their Source, which needs nothing, they were free to value and celebrate their mates. However, there was no investment in the man, but rather a calm willingness to enjoy him.

The Source can use the heart or brain to care, if it wants to, but it does not need to. When a woman's brain or heart rules, having to care is often central to the persona she believes she is. After a lifetime of believing that she needs to care for everything around her or that she needs to give her emotionality to her mate, her job or her extended family, a woman is understandably depleted. Giving energy from an expansive system without having it grounded in a concentrating or collecting system will deplete the body. Imbalanced giving from the heart for a woman can eventually lead to the physical symptoms of cystic breasts or even breast cancer.

One adage from business is applicable here: Pay yourself first. Put your energy into your Source first. Then, if so moved, decide where to spend it.

Many women are shocked to realize, when centered within their Source, how little they care about so much. The stronger she becomes, the more peace will emanate into her surroundings. A relaxed, calm woman is different from one who is stressed and exhausted. It leaves a woman free to treat herself with all the care she has lavished on those around her in the service of survival.

Organization is often easy to see in patients. One fellow was talking about his wife. He said that she was not being kind to him and that she ignored him. He was asked whether he felt that she should always be open to him. He said she should because he was always thinking about her, always willing to be there for her, so he expected the same thing.

I suggested that if she felt it was not good for her to open to him at a given time, it was being true to herself to not force it. My reasoning was that, if their positions were reversed, I would want him to stand up for what he felt was good for him to her. However, it was clear that he felt that what was good for him was for her to open to him.

So what does one do when one person's definitions include how the other party must behave?

We talked about needs and how necessary it is to fulfill our own. I mentioned something I'd noticed: When men want, our energy becomes like a lightning bolt. I asked him if he would feel like opening if the person demanding it was throwing bolts. It would be silly to open to someone demanding it or needing it. How much energy would they take, and would they ever be satisfied once they knew that they could bully for it? Or whine for it? Plainly, he was operating from a young layer that had needs. But only he could meet those needs because only he knew and had experienced the losses that created them.

He was coming from his hard brain, believing that the definition of wife included opening to him on demand. A freer definition would allow him to self-validate, that is, open his heart energy to himself when he needed it rather than getting someone else's energy involved in his body. If he was always thinking about her, was he going deeper and looking at the part of himself that she represented?

She represented to him both his inner female and his heart energy. As he was able to better determine from which beliefs his needs were stemming, he was better able to differentiate between his head and his heart. As he became more receptive to himself, he was honoring his inner female (yin = receptive) and had less need for his wife's validation. His organization evolved from being hard-brained—i.e., definition- and belief-centered—and soft-hearted, feeling victimized, to being open-hearted and full. When a man has his Source full, he is self-loving and self-fulfilling.

Not surprisingly, his wife felt like being closer to him the less needy he was for her energy and attention. Which is more attractive? A person who needs another to behave in a certain way in order to feel okay, or a person who finds joy and peace within himself and in his own company, and would rather be alone than in a situation that was draining?

Another patient, a young woman, said that she felt bad for not having sex with her boyfriend, because she did not feel like a good girlfriend. It seemed as if her brain was giving her a definition of what a "good" girlfriend did. When asked what was true for her from the position of her Source, she said that she did not feel sexual at the time, as she was healing from sexual trauma in her past. She needed to offer her brain a new definition of a good girlfriend: one who takes care of her issues however she needs to in order to be a more complete woman and have a more complete relationship. After she experienced the Source treatment, she was amazed how clear her options were. Asked if she still felt like a bad girlfriend, she smiled, shrugged, and said that he was welcome to feel whatever he wished; she was taking good care of herself and was peaceful with her decision to have sex only when she felt that she could be present for it. She would not, and from her womb could not, have sex merely because her mind's persona and her soft heart dictated that it was what a good girlfriend did.

Another quality the Source has is patience. It can wait and let something grow slowly. That is why the mind's learned pace is so antithetical to the womb. Going slow ultimately makes everything sweeter and more tender. It makes things gentle. The womb nurtures through patience and ruthlessness. It is ruthless about protecting whatever is in its field. The end result of becoming Source-centered is that the womb begins treating the woman as its child.

In other species the qualities of the womb are easy to see. We have all heard about mother bears fighting off huge males in defense of their cubs.

And when the cubs are grown and able to fend for themselves, a feat that requires tremendous patience, she drives them off. That is ruthlessness, patience and ruthlessness again. It is necessary if the mother bear and her cubs are to survive.

Some people mistake ruthlessness for callousness or cruelty. Callousness is the quality of being unfeeling; cruelty equals sadism. The womb feels more than a man and most women can imagine, but it does not choose, in its ruthlessness, to let certain feelings come within its field. It has no political correctness and does not believe that everything must be experienced. Stress, obsession, fear, etc.—it simply does not meld with those vibrations.

The womb is a woman's connection to all worlds, to the Source of all Creation. Within its field is an extra-dimensional space. The farther a woman gets from it, the harder it is for her to be healthy. The head is about as far from the uterus as you can get.

As on an old phonographic turntable or a merry-go-round, the farther we get from the Source, the more likely we are to spin off. Only at the center does each revolution involve merely facing a different direction.

CHAPTER THREE

THE STRIFE BETWEEN SEXES

It is my premise that only one system in men and one system in women is capable and designed for the second-by-second assessment of life situations, and an implementation of an internally loving, non-partisan response. When each system has the energy it requires, we are healed of whatever ails us, and we are well.

In women, the womb is designed by the Ki of Humanity, Creation, to be the center of a balanced consciousness. The uterus is the place where a woman can find her Source. Likewise, I have found that in men, it is the heart that is the Source. However, in both men and women, the respective systems must be full of conscious life energy to be an effective Source for our identities. Without our consciousness in these respective places, we find ourselves interacting with the worlds (inner and outer) from systems unable to receive energy, and from places that were designed to apprehend only certain wavelengths or aspects of the whole.

The systems from which we usually organize consciousness are designed to implement rather than create. When we put them in the role of Creator or of decider, they are understandably at a loss. This is because they can only judge from a relative point of view. The hearts of men and the wombs of women are designed to receive full energy and information from the world and choose how, if at all, to respond. They are the only systems capable of doing so with the totality of our awareness.

In my first 10 years of practice, I noticed two things almost without exception: women were the most depleted in the areas below the navel, and men were depleted in the area above the diaphragm. The struggles that I and my patients went through in order to strengthen the weak systems were monumental. Almost everyone was balanced when they left my office; few stayed that way for more than a few hours or days. Patients could be relieved of their symptoms relatively quickly, but the weakness remained. In those days I looked at the weakness as a sign of the Base Condition—i.e., a condition that the body was born with or that was the original deficiency.

Over time, I learned that women responded better to gentler dosage treatments, with explanations about what was being treated and why. When I did not explain what I was doing, the treatment was not as effective as when I did. By dosage I mean the depth and stimulation of both needling and acupressure. Men responded better to wordless treatments with stronger dosages. And yet the general areas of weakness remained.

It fascinated me that men and women required such different approaches. It also caught my imagination to discover for myself that healing was about giving what was required.

Beliefs and treatments evolve. I began to notice that patients' personalities would change when energy was finally invited to sit where it had been weakest. As the weak systems began to heal, patients were no longer troubled by the things they had been obsessed with. Problems and neuroses became less pronounced and then ceased to be issues. The speed of progress depended on how chronically imbalanced the systems were.

Then, while working with a female patient one day, I discovered a natural progression in my treatment. Instead of just guiding her life energy below her navel with moxa, pressure or needles, I verbally also guided her consciousness to her womb. The results were instantaneous and shockingly powerful. She said that she could not ever recall being so much herself—so relaxed, so calm, so untroubled by anything. Her life was just the same, but she was not in the same place in relationship to it. It was as if she had two years of treatment in half an hour. I recall a tremendous amount of laughter filling that session.

When I treated and verbally guided a person's conscious energy to the Source, almost every patient experienced a similar result, and that amazed me. When I first guided a man's energy into his Source, the result was the same. A tremendous amount of tension simply disappeared. He could not recall ever being so inwardly still and peaceful. There was wonder on his face, and he could not stop smiling.

It is wondrous to discover this place we all have. That sense of peace is easily lost in today's world. It seems a cruel joke unless we learn how to consciously go to that place. It is a worthy pursuit for any person: to discover one's internal Life Will and interact with it as a concrete relationship.

Humans today are taught to organize their life energy in ways that are opposed to our natural way. "Natural way" means that everything in our bodies is designed for a specific range of vibration and functions. Some systems are designed to hold energy and others to use or let it flow. And certain systems, in men and in women, are meant to guide us. They are the Source of our lives. I contend that these certain systems, different in men and women, were designed by the energy of Creation itself to guide and protect us, and have the innate wisdom to do so. It is these systems that I call the Source.

The Source in women is their uterine system, not, as is so often claimed within the New Age movement, the heart. The womb is where a woman finds peace, where everything is always fine, her home and her place of power. The womb as a place of conscious power is not a new theory, but outside of shamanism it seems to be given little attention. In later chapters the uterine system will be defined further, as it does not include only the physical womb. Women with radical hysterectomies still have uterine energy, as do women after menopause.

The key seems to be that certain anatomical areas in men and women are able to collect vast amounts of energy. We experience that collection, when it has been allowed to take place, as the emotional state of being well.

The Source in men is the heart system, as the seat of joy. Joy, to the Eastern Medical way of thinking, is more than just delight; it is the capacity of the human being to participate in life openly and without reservation. Joy is the ability to apprehend any circumstance with acceptance and full participation. Joy, in other words, is the ability to feel alive. This feeling is present even when a loved one dies. When we allow ourselves to connect to our Source, we feel all the sadness mixed with the gratitude that we shared so much with that person. It is a complete experience, and as such it constitutes joy.

In practice and in life, men most often organize their energies around two areas. The first is the head, and the second is the genitals, what men jokingly refer to as the little head. Women organize around the head or the heart or, in fewer cases, around the genitals. It is necessary to differentiate between the womb and the genitals because the mind or heart can often control the genitals; neither can control the womb.

I have found that balanced men perceive from a full and receptive heart. Balanced women perceive from a womb full of life energy. The other places capable of organizing energies ought to be mere options. As I have come to understand yin and yang theory, the receptive, or yin, center for a man is his heart; his genitals and brain are expansive, or yang. A woman's receptive place is her womb. Her heart and brain are expansive in comparison.

The Source in both men and women must be receptive, both to our own energies and to the vibrations of life energy from the universe. If we organize ourselves first from an expansive (yang) place, we become dependent on only our own energies as well as external rewards. We then find ourselves trapped in a state of activity and speed rather than rest. When we organize from a receptive (yin) place, we gather the energies of the larger universe and use our own expansive energy only to guide the journey.

Control without being guided and grounded by true power becomes domination, as it is driven by emptiness. Power without the wisdom to direct it becomes either stagnant or fuels unconscious, destructive and ineffective actions. We can all see the result of power without wisdom in the daily political actions of our countries.

Our Sources, when full, have the ability to rest within their power and then, when expansion or interaction becomes desirable, use our will and intent in the world in the most skillful, elegant ways imaginable.

Systems not designed to guide us in our totality often, through experience and habit, learn to take energies from weaker systems. Taking energy creates symptoms, personae, beliefs and internal pressure because aspects of our bodies are trying to fight with other aspects that are us as well. Those symptoms are often projected onto our external lives. It is no coincidence that our closest external relationships resemble the relationship we have internally with parts of self.

Healing can take place when the Source contains a preponderance of our life energy. From that place of fullness, the Source can easily distribute the necessary energies throughout the body. However, the judgment of how much energy, and to which system it needs to be sent, have to be the decisions of the Source. Only then is the decision coming from a place that is capable of receiving all the information, both seen and unseen, without partisanship.

When we do not organize our lives around our Sources' wills, the imbalances we develop are evident through the speeds (vibrations) of our other systems.

HEAT AND SPEED

In my basic Japanese acupuncture training, one ancient doctor was mentioned again and again. Sowada Sensei's premise was that all disease was a mismanagement of heat. Too much heat in certain meridians or areas of the body, and not enough in others, was the cause of all ills. Perhaps more suited to today's world is the concept of speed. Too much speed often creates heat. If an organ or system is constantly made to move at a speed it was not designed for, or is not given enough rest or sustenance, imbalance of the entire organism can ensue.

In traditional Eastern medicine, each season has its own laws of health care. To behave year round the same way, be it through work, diet, exercise, emotional activity, etc., will invite illness. The speed that is healthy for an individual in the summer might be devastating in the winter; activities that seem fine in the fall might be weakening in the spring. For very sensitive people, whether it is cloudy or sunny, humid or dry may make a huge difference in the optimal organization of their life energy. It is important to understand that we are also made, initially, in the climate in which we are gestated. We have a base climate internally that we would do well to be aware of in terms of diet, lifestyle, etc. This base climate is the internal balance of heat, humidity, dryness, cold, etc. in which our systems can best rest and heal in. This balance is also experienced as emotional and physical peace. In essence, we have a base speed, if we can remember or discover it, in which we will feel perfectly at ease. However, this is not a static speed.

In our world we move too fast. We even slow down too fast. Most things we do are judged by speed. Faster is better in the workplace, in the sporting arenas, in almost everything. Not in the body, though. Within the body there is a time for speed, but it is designed to be infrequent. Speed comes from taxing the adrenals, from triggering the fight-flight reflex. Adrenaline is meant to be released when our physical existence is threatened, not when a deadline looms, when someone says something nasty, or when we get cut off while driving. Any triggering of adrenaline leads to depletion. With rest and time we can renew our adrenal energies. There is rarely, however, time for true rest in our lives. Indeed, most of us do not even know that it is required.

When we move at our specific, variable speed as judged by the Source, what we can call Life Speed, everything is right. Instead of racing for that bus, it is just there when we arrive. We walk into a place just as the love of our life arrives. We miss that careening cab. In other words, when we move at our life-appropriate speed, we are on time for our life. We weave past what we do not want and are on time for what we do.

When we move at a speed dictated by any system other than our Source, we are in the wrong place at the wrong time. Or rather, we are in dysfunctional, dualistic time, i.e., the right place for dysfunctional events. We miss the bus, we leave moments before our love walks in, and we walk in front of that cab. If we are lucky, our bodies give us aches and pains to slow us down in an attempt to return us to our speed of life. Looked at in this light, is it not conceivable that an aching back or a migraine may have saved your life?

Heat and speed are not, and cannot ever be, static. Flux is necessary because our bodies and spirits are interacting with constantly changing variables. One needs to be able to sense what is appropriate for each moment, and that, of course, means the ability to be in the present. All life manifests in every moment, and so it follows that what is right for the whole of each of us can only be decided second by second. With that premise, from where we judge what is appropriate becomes paramount.

Let us examine the different internal locations from which we manage or organize our life energy.

The brain can focus only on one subject at a time and is largely preoccupied with its safety in the external world. When the mind is dominant, we can judge, choose and act based only on past experiences, ideas, loyalties and memories of teachings. This view may or may not result in a helpful experience for the entire body.

The speed of the heart can judge based on feelings—that is, the emotional content of the issue. Heart energy is receptive in men, as it collects energy, and expansive in women, as it sends energy out. Thus heart energy is often experienced differently for men and women. The speed of the energy-full heart is the most effective speed a man can aspire to; it is from this speed that he can direct his life energy most effectively, as the situation demands. It is the place of power, the Source, for men because it is the only place designed to collect and contain all of our life energy. Putting our life energy elsewhere creates a void, a vacuum that needs to be filled from external sources. These external sources can be religion, relationships with women or men, money, image, success, cars, teachers or philosophies—that is, anything we can use to give us a sense of love, joy and fulfillment. As long as we are dependent on the external world for these things, we are slaves to the speed of need. When we can find our internal needs and fulfill them, we can interact with the world from a position of fullness and satisfaction rather than need. In balanced men, the full, receptive heart can lead to an intuitive sense of what is appropriate to give or receive in a given moment.

Men and women often operate on a different set of perceptions. In general, men are less physically sensitive than women. We are also more fragile in that once we notice we are hurt, we are very hurt. There are, or course, numerous exceptions, but men have a bit more leeway in our physical options, in that we can handle or ignore physical shocks with seemingly greater ease.

Men have more surface expansive energy and thus are more concerned and interested in external reality. Men somatically feel less inside, so our focus tends to be in the external field.

It is the intent of the huge surface energy in men to create and maintain external circumstances that benefit feminine energy, that is, everything that life comes from.

Men's expansive energy is intended to create a field of possibility and confidence. Masculine energy, when balanced, full and strong, can create a place for feminine energy, our own or that of others, to look inward, knowing confidently that it is safe. Although we may not have the option, as men, of growing another life within us and nurturing it from our bodies, what masculine energy does have is the responsibility of making sure that feminine energy and the children of their union are peaceful, happy and safe. To that end, we are built to be warriors. We are strong and have a built-in desire to interact physically and spiritually. We have a willingness to give our bodies over to a good cause. We also have, as we grow, a desire to measure ourselves against elements in the world in order to see what will yield. We men also need to know where we are in relation to other men. It can be described as fighting, but that is not the underlying intent. Testing ourselves is part of being men. The ineffective thing we have done is to translate the need to measure ourselves against others with fighting. And we have made winning paramount, regardless of cost, instead of questioning where the directives for fighting originate.

When we fight each other, we do so at the directives of the brain, the heart or the genitals. They may not know what it feels like to be the recipient, but bodies (the embodiment of feminine energy) do. After years of martial arts, I can honestly say that I have hurt people and I have been hurt. Either way, a loss took place.

Competition and winning seem to be accepted and encouraged in today's social world of business, politics and entertainment, but our inner world is solely our society.

Any violence, directed internally or externally, is felt by the body. Internal competition is the same as brutalizing ourselves. That's why we must, as a first step, be fair to ourselves. Do we say things and treat ourselves as we would our best friends or even strangers? Or are we harder on ourselves and those closest to us, and nicer to those more distant relations? Were we fair, we would demand that we treat and speak to ourselves as kindly as we do anyone in our fields (whoever is getting our best).

The impetus for men to fight is useful if it can be translated into acting effectively in the service of something gentle and sweet (but strong), thus tempering and educating our tendencies to dominate and destroy. That is using our consciousness and our desire to serve in order to learn the will of our own Sources.

Perhaps this offers an insight into why boys are often so entranced with knights. It is only as adults that we learn how corrupt they were as men; the initial fantasy of a man serving his Lord (Source) with integrity and chastity is a beautiful one. Chaste, in Old French, means pure and simple. We, as men, require clarity in order to act with integrity. We require action leading to wholeness. As men, our internal life will be perceived in our external world. Whatever we are going through within our bodies, we will perceive as "our take" on our surroundings or situation.

We men can be heroic only if we serve heroic ideals and logic. It is a useful question: Are our core beliefs heroic toward ourselves and all life?

If we act with integrity and joy, our hearts are strong and we are renewed. If we habitually act from any other position, we eventually lose our health and our birthright as men. Honor is central to a healthy male organization. It is what we honor that has to be looked at long and hard. If we honor and give our loyalty to imbalanced thoughts, ideas or beliefs, we ourselves become imbalanced. It can be a long time, however, before we notice it. Thus how we define and act out our beliefs must be open to our own ability to edit and choose. We keep those things that make life more beautiful. We meticulously discard habits, loyalties and beliefs that keep us in a place of competing with life, which is represented internally by the Sources.

In competition with life, life will win.

When we, as men, learn to gather our energy to our hearts and open ourselves, we realize that there is not so much to fear, not so much that we cannot handle. We feel very present to our energy, our power, and do not want to waste it on things that bring discomfort to us or anyone else. We learn to care for ourselves, and that field of caring extends into our everyday lives. As the I Ching says:

Preponderance of the Great: Everything furthers.

The full, open heart is the place where men can consistently be balanced and at peace.

From our expansive natures men get the impulse to protect, create safety and spark life. Those are yang functions. We can also get a tiny glimpse of male yin energy from the prostate. Men often put too much competitive, needy or judgmental emphasis—which is injurious energy, speed and vibration—onto sexuality. That translates into heat and speed for our genitals, and the prostate is eventually depleted. Men and women both have masculine and feminine energies. Masculine energy, yang, must have worthy causes to pursue. Feminine energy, yin, must have periods of quiet and nurturing to remain strong.

For a woman, whatever is happening in the external world is of relatively little importance. It is her connection to her full womb that is essential for balance. In this way she is in contact with the Source of all life, and through that connection she will be able to influence masculine energy and society toward an external balance.

Women, when balanced, have more internal expansive energy. They can more easily recover from emotional shocks. This gift of steadiness and internal power is women's birthright. It is by giving more attention to their inner world, through their wombs, that women can begin to gain some inkling of their vast power and connection to all living things.

Girls are often taught to be softhearted and giving and to take care of a home or a mate or a child, without being taught that heart energy is merely one option. Being giving is not meant to become an identity. They come into their power (menarche) without ever knowing that the flow of their power has just crested, and they are taught by society to remain separated from it. The attitude many women have toward true personal power is often identical to their relationship to their wombs, body image and menstrual cycles. The womb is the physical manifestation of the energy of Creation. Girls can learn that bleeding means something beyond the womb merely shedding its lining. Pain or PMS is a result of an energy-depleted female system.

Some young women fear menstruation, as it can be painful or messy. So can power used ineffectively. Women can spend years in terror of becoming pregnant. Fear feeds the brain. That stress does nothing to bring a young woman into accord with her birthright. After all, if power is just energy and a woman has more energy in her womb when pregnant, would she not long for it even as she feared it?

The confusion is based on the knowledge (usually unconscious) that life energy belongs in the womb. This is countered by the taught belief that the only acceptable time, as dictated by male-dominated religions, societies or families, to allow energy in the womb is during pregnancy. Thus, young women never learn about womb-based energy. Under pressure from the masculine, it has been demonstrated to girls by women for untold generations that the only purpose for a womb is childbearing. Unfortunately, it has also been modeled for girls to choose a mate from their heads or hearts or genitals in order to procure safety. If her worldview stems from a place where she can only use the limited choices she has witnessed, any choice she can make will be survival-based.

The reasons women tacitly (and unconsciously) teach their daughters to bow to this masculine (yang) domination and subjugation is because both genders can and do enact this enslavement of yin internally first. A woman's masculine-patterned consciousness can be as emotionally brutal on the woman herself as any bad relationship. This patterning is survival-based, and is, I believe, due to historic trauma to the feminine energy in the human sphere.

We can examine history to find a myriad of examples of when womb-based women still had freedom and autonomy. They were the midwives, the women who knew herbs and healing, and who lived with nature. These women were rounded up as animals and tortured or burnt as witches. The lucky (or unlucky) ones were enslaved by a paternal society that saw womb-based women as the unrepentant descendants of Lilith and Eve, the embodiment of temptation, the fall from grace, and sin. Any suppression and punishment of womb energy was considered both a civic and religious duty. And this is just the most basic example of more than five thousand years of using the feminine.

After generations of this treatment, our external world has given both women and men good reason to avoid putting power in the feminine. Having lost the feminine elders and their knowledge in a spectacular ongoing display of masculine distrust of the unknown and uncontrollable, we also lost contact with their vast wisdom.

The masculine energy that enacted matricide also succeeded in destroying its link to its own inner feminine. Because the masculine is outwardly directed, the need for the lost feminine has turned us all, men and women alike, into some version of a lost child searching for "mommy" in the outside world.

A girl would need to know all this in learning to grow into who she authentically is as a woman, and to protect her life energy from being pigeonholed by an external world dominated by twisted masculine energy. By twisted, I mean that we can all name a multitude of examples of masculine energy acting in the world in a sick and imbalanced way. We are offered very few balanced views of healthy men and women. When well balanced, masculine energy does not dominate, need or demand. Our natural masculine and feminine energies have become twisted by religious, gender-based, historic and social definitions of how men and women should act.

For example, who could say what a young woman with a balanced view of her own power would choose in her life? What choice would she make if each system was relaxed and already fulfilled and she had her own speed, instead of the speed dictated from peers or society? What choice might she make if she was aware that the womb is designed to hold all of her energy whether she is pregnant or not?

Anorexia, for example, is a disease whose premise is based on the brain deciding that being beautiful equals being skinny. It is to the mind, then, logical that the thinner a girl looks, the more lovely she is. The brain commandeers energy and changes how the girl perceives. The brain can change how she feels and how she thinks she feels, and can even change how she sees her reflection in a mirror. It is no surprise that when young women follow their brains, they stop menstruating (or never start). They have been seduced away from their own power, without ever feeling it, by the belief that a woman has to be 20 pounds underweight to be desirable and loved. When a woman has her energy in her womb, she knows that she is loved and needs no one outside for validation. She may always want validation, but she will not need it.

When women operate from their expansive and giving hearts, they often deplete themselves. This depletion occurs for several reasons. Among them is that the directive to give comes from an expansive, outwardly concerned place. Women can give energy from their hearts because the brain tells them it is what they should do and who they are.

Based on the brain's static identification of who the woman is, the heart will be required to behave in certain ways. The mind can tell her that it is the only way to prove that she is kind and loving, and after all, who would not want to be perceived that way? It can also tell her that not spending her emotional energy on something means that she is cold, or give her some other negative mental definition of her persona if she does not spend her heart energy. Since the heart in a woman is designed to implement Source decisions and cannot collect energy, she ends up "leaking" her life energy out through her heart.

If a woman identifies herself with the heart, she is also going to leak energy. This depletion will occur because she will believe that she is her sentiment, that she is her caring, rather than having sentiment and caring be options that she can use. There will be no way for her to find solid ground here, only further loss. She will not be able to commune with the Earth, because she will be keeping all her energy occupied above her navel. It is in grounding with the lower vibrations of the womb, this communing, that a woman replenishes and heals herself. Keeping an energetic organization centered around the heart is ultimately draining and compromising for a woman, just as keeping an energetic organization around the genitals is for a man. It is not necessarily a physical death, but a spiritual one.

The fact that men and women both organize around our expansive brains is another reason for the state we find our world in. For if women organize around their brains, they are just as limited as men in that organization, and we remain deprived of the true wisdom of the Earth. And the Earth is the Source of us all.

For women, coming from the heart keeps them from accessing the universal wisdom of the womb, a place from which we have all come. The womb judges based on its connection with the very energy of Creation itself.

It is indeed the only system capable of physical creation at the quantum level, a matchless accomplishment from time immemorial.

It is an obvious truth, but consider that everyone who has ever lived was born from a womb, and, since our species continues, was born well. The overall perfection of the womb's work is there for all to see. Most people have their features in appropriate places, and digits and organs and bodies that work. The miracle of fetal development is awesome, created layer by layer with a complexity and grace finer than any symphony. Infants operated on in utero do not develop scars. That is because the womb is the earthly manifestation of Creation itself.

When a woman puts her identity into the womb, she is standing in the place in which life is created. She has, to use a religious metaphor, returned to Eden. We each, second by second, continue to nibble at the apple of flawed knowledge and pull our energy away from the Garden. To continue with this metaphor, to our body, the snake is the mind that perpetually seduces or takes our Life Energy into an obsessive, survival-based paradigm. Owing to the good-bad, win-lose, joy-guilt, freedom-shame clauses that have become well-worn neural pathways in our brains, which we notice as various stresses, it is difficult to even conceive of a powerful, relaxed, neutral inner Source.

The decisions coming from a Source-centered woman are invariably calm, humorous, wise and certain. With her energy in her Source, a woman has the option of using either the heart or the mind to carry out or to accentuate her decisions. That is the smoothest way for a woman to use her expansive systems. Once all the energy is in the womb, a woman can decide what she wants to do, if anything, about any subject.

For example, if a woman is faced with a choice, what she decides will be very different depending on from where, internally, she is making the decision. From her Source, a woman can judge whether that decision even needs to be made and, if so, if it will be most effectively channeled through the mind, heart or genitals. The womb is the only place in a woman that can choose perfectly how to engage any other system in her body without wounding or depleting it. The key is that when the womb's energetic reservoir is full, it takes care of everything.

One young woman I worked with was in her final year of nursing school. I treated her through her exams, and two weeks before the end of the year she came in completely unbalanced. She was having anxiety attacks, insomnia and nausea. I had already guided her though a uterine treatment, and I asked her how much energy (time) she was spending with her womb. She reported that she had been too overwhelmed to focus on her Source. During the treatment we worked on collecting her consciousness back to the womb. The following week she came in with no symptoms at all. She seemed relaxed and quiet. She said that she still had a lot of work to do, but it was all getting done rather easily, and anyway, she felt strangely unconcerned. She was still doing the same amount of work, but it was stemming from a place of peace and relaxation. In other words, she was letting her Source use her mind. It was amazing to me how she had shifted so radically so quickly. By paying more attention to her womb and less to her work, more was getting done, and in a smoother, easier way. She had even gone out for a drink with friends the night before our appointment. When brain-centered, she would have never given herself the pleasure, only the pressure.

If a woman comes from her mind without the Source's wisdom guiding things, she will be using the body (life, womb) to carry out plans based on past experiences and imagined projections. That is, her life energy will be spent by a brain that tries to act in a venue (life) that it cannot, and was not designed to, fully perceive.

If she chooses from her Source to use her heart to carry out the decision, she is using her emotion to experience the decisions made by the womb. She can flow life energy from her Source to her heart and thus experience her judgment in an emotional way. It is based on choice. That choice will lead to a much different experience from the response offered from the woman's typical organization that demands her acting from an emotional persona—i.e., getting stuck in the learned need for women to be emotionally soft, volatile or vulnerable. The key issue is choice. Women can still experience the full range of their emotional capacities, perhaps an even fuller range, but they are not compelled to. The power within the choice of whether to open the heart or not cannot be overstated.

The speed of the womb is characterized by the qualities of being unhurried, peaceful, secure, humorous, sweet, wise and certain. Calmness emanates up through the woman's body when she has collected her energy into her Source. And the Source in both sexes is ruthless in protecting its various systems and persona, but in a deft, easy way that excludes no parts of self.

Another woman came into the office crying about the state of her relationship. The diagnosis broke down as follows: She was coming from the speed of her heart, emotion, qualified by the viewpoint of her head, logic. She could not, based on projecting past experience into a static perception of the future, see how her heart could ever feel happy. When guided to let her womb have enough life energy to actually communicate, she suddenly giggled. It was infectious, and after we both stopped laughing, I asked her what she had come to. She said, "From my womb, I just don't care." After that treatment, whenever she got upset, she would drop her energy, and that liberating feeling of not caring would return. After the session she was worried that she would become callous and heartless. Her experience, however, in coming from her Source was that she could clearly see what she wanted to get involved in and what she did not, and she had no guilt for "not going there"—that is, not giving her energy away to the experience, man, etc. She found herself joyful, certain and happy. She could give without needing validation, because she had begun to give from a place of fullness.

When we organize our personalities around systems that are not meant to hold positions of decision, we become what we can learn to recognize as our false selves. Our consciousness is not false to its own understanding, but it is unavoidably false to the rest of our body. This is because it does not consider the body as having its own distinct consciousness and experience.

If we are organized from an expansive place, we have created a persona based on projection. We can only project parts of ourselves through expansive energy.

With concentrating energy, we are all of ourselves. As we concentrate our energies into our Source, we are gathering and collecting life energy, all of our pieces of energy, every bit of ourselves. Our false selves, together with our shadow energies,[2] brought under the guidance of our true self (the Source), brings us to completion.

As we are guided by our Sources we can act with our conscious energy and our shadow energy together. We will no longer need to concern ourselves with disowned parts because to the Source, parts of self are a simple matter of energy that can be collected into the Source regardless of

---

[2] Shadow energies are the parts of our identities we disown. Usually they are the polar opposites of anything we feel strongly about and identify with. If we love something and also hate it, but refuse to own our hatred, that energy of hatred goes into our shadow.

how the brain or heart (for women) labels them. To the Source, energy is energy and it will accept energy that we have labeled bad just as easily as that which we have labeled good. If nothing is disowned, nothing needs to act out or commandeer energy.

Many pregnant women find themselves moving at womb-speed. Women can allay their own fears by asking their Sources to guide them, to remember the joy, unconcern, power, humor, peace and playfulness they may have experienced during pregnancy. Women who have difficult pregnancies typically have very strong identities in either the heart or mind. The persona in charge will not release its hold (energy), no matter the needs of the womb at that time.

Acting and living from the speed of our guiding Source puts us in integrity, which is wholeness. Coming from any other system immediately creates a shift to a dualistic paradigm, which in turn leads to winners and losers, in terms of systems, energy and how we perceive our world. As our brains rule, we operate at a speed that depletes our other systems. When women let their hearts rule, the same depletion occurs, as it does when men or women allow their genitals to lead.

Only the Source can discern, instant by instant, how to organize and deploy energy so that no system is drained. Symptoms of stress, be they physical, emotional or spiritual, are created when we organize around an expansive system. Once we learn how to ask our Source what our perfect speed is, we are on our way to health. When we learn to sincerely give our Source our attention and ask it to decide on our best speed and relate to it as we would any other critically important relationship in our lives, we will be healed.

CHAPTER FOUR

SEXUAL CIRCULATION OF LIFE ENERGY

When men and women engage in sexual intercourse, they can cause life energy to grow or they can use sex in an imbalanced way that in turn leads to depletion.[3] In other words, it can be used in the service or disservice of both. Imbalanced sex is when one partner uses the other to get life energy, leaving the partner who did not receive depleted.

Being in service and using occur in every facet of existence, including intimate relationships. Sex merely offers one example of this. Many people use others emotionally, often with the excuse (and belief) that they are actually in service to them. Sometimes couples trade. He will use her for sex, and she will use him for emotional or financial security. She will use him for sex, and he will use her to get back at his mother. He will use her to make him feel, and she will use him to feel useful or needed. When operating outside of our Sources, we can believe we are in service to something in the outside world. However, because of our internal organization, we find ourselves using what we think we are in service to. Thus it is important that we have some idea of what we believe we are in service to, and what we are using. The list of tacit agreements is as varied as relationships. We are

---

[3] This next section is based on work with heterosexual men and women. The circulation of Life Energy during homosexual or lesbian sex is there, of course, but is different.

touching specifically on sex because it can be a powerful way to rebuild lost life energy, and it can also be a way to avoid losing life energy.

Traditional Eastern medicine says that men lose energy when they ejaculate and that women lose energy during menstruation, childbirth and nursing. Both theories are true to a point. Anything, if done to excess or in an unclear or incomplete fashion, can cause a loss of energy. However, if there is a consensual sexual act in service of one's own life energy grounded in the Source, it can strengthen both parties.

A note of caution: The following is a powerful energetic exercise. Though condoms can inhibit some sensation, this is preferable to an unplanned pregnancy. I have treated two women who were infertile for a number of years before trying this exercise. They both are now mothers.

If a woman gathers her energy in her womb and desires sexual intimacy with a man, and he gathers his energy in his heart, opens it and wants to have sex too, then a great exchange of life energy can take place. This is how it is done.

The woman takes the man inside her. She lets her energy flow up her spine into her heart. This is her using her heart in the service of her womb. From her heart, breasts, nipples, she gives that energy to the man.

He takes that energy into his nipples, breasts, focuses it deep within his heart, and brings it back to his spine. The energy flows down, focuses in his prostate, flows out through his penis into the woman's womb, and the cycle begins again. This is a man using his penis in the service of his heart.

It is important that the woman initiates the flow. The importance lies in the clarity that she is not being forced, by mere entry, to flow her energy to her partner. As the one being entered, it is important that her gift of energy be voluntary. The man needs to open his heart to allow the energy in.

This exercise cannot be done alone. Sexual communion between the Sources is an awesome, healing experience. If the woman gives the energy and it is lost somewhere between a man's chest and penis, she gets nothing back, and the circuit is broken. If a man gives his energy and it does not return, the circuit is also broken. If the connection is broken, then it is just a sexual act. While fun for the system in control, sex without a conscious connection of life energy between the Sources can deplete our energy.

It is interesting to use the service and using template as a window into our own internal organization whenever there is an exchange of energy, be it at work, at play or even on the bus. We can use any opportunity to question whether we are engaged in service to our Source. The question is, Are we creating a win-win situation or is someone going to lose? When we lose, what we are losing besides the evident issue is energy. And we often end up putting our bodies in situations and around people who are quite willing to use us. We can request from our consciousness a simple benchmark: that we put ourselves only in situations we would happily let our best-loved friend or young child be in. If our body is a precious friend to us, do we put it in positions where it is unsafe or unhappy? After all, any decision made by the consciousness has its consequences played out upon the body. As we take loving care of our body, where we put it, and in whose company, we are attempting to create a win-win for all of ourselves. This is the Source's viewpoint reached through mental discipline, intent, and will.

Here are some questions we can ask of ourselves in order to become aware of energy leaks: Are we doing something because we want to receive energy or because we have lost energy? Am I mad (hard heart) because I got my feelings hurt? Did my hurt feelings make me lose energy? Am I saying that hurtful thing because I feel that I have lost energy and want to get it back? If I lose energy through thoughts or emotions, how do I get it back? Do I find someone to take it from, or do I pillage one of my own systems to make the dominant persona feel better? What do I habitually do to stop losing energy?

Of course, focusing all our energy into the Source will stop us from losing energy, but it is always useful to know more about ourselves until such time as our Sources have absorbed all of our personae. In the final analysis, all personae are merely life energy.

It is interesting to see what we externally choose to lose energy to, because it is a reflection of what we are doing internally. Our relationships in our everyday lives mirror our mind's relationship with yin and yang energy within ourselves. Our treatment of our friends and enemies is exactly the same as how some of our systems treat other systems. If the heart hates the brain, it will show up in our life. Sometimes this is metaphoric, but more often it is beautifully concrete.

Clinically, with gay patients, it has usually been necessary to ask them to pay special conscious attention to the opposite-sex energy within them, as well as to their same-sex energy. It is not uncommon in treatment to have them go through their belief about men, and then about women, and see if the logic is biased. How does this man feel about femininity, and how does he feel about masculinity? Are both options available for him to express? Or does he deny an aspect of himself?

The same holds true for lesbians. Does this woman like masculine energy or feminine? Does she like both or are her options limited because she is not accepting a part of herself? This is not to say that lesbians ignore their feminine side and gays ignore their masculine. The weakness, neglect or over-involvement with the masculine for women, and the feminine for men, is an imbalance that exists in most of us, but often it is more confusing for homosexual people because their identity is tied up with societal beliefs and stigma.

Heterosexuals usually act out their feelings about their inner opposite on their primary partner. Gay men and lesbian women may also do this, but because the energy of their partner is intrinsically similar, it may not be as obvious.

Regardless of one's sexual orientation, developing a kind internal dialogue is a good start at commencing a stronger relationship with our inner energies. As we are nicer to ourselves, it is interesting to see that our external relationships, especially those closest to us, also become sweeter. Which leads to the conjecture that perhaps everything we experience emotionally, as happening to us in the outside world, is a primary projection mirroring how we treat ourselves in the inner world.

I was treating a woman in her fifties who suffered from chronic fatigue syndrome, Lyme disease, fibromyalgia and a host of other symptoms. She was a lesbian, although she had been married to a man for many years prior to when we worked together. In the course of the treatments she began to speak about her ex-husband. They had made an agreement early on in their marriage that she could not refuse him sex, no matter what was going on. Toward the end of their marriage, they were bitter toward one another, yet still having sex. Her illnesses started in the year following their divorce. One day she said, "I can't imagine what he was pumping into me."

That statement stayed with me. Over the years many patients have reported that during oral sex, the taste of semen changed dramatically depending on the man's physical or mental health. It led me to theorize that men can expel toxins through their semen, even as women do through menstruation. This toxicity, in semen especially, can injure a woman's health if she does not have enough life energy in her uterus. Semen can live for several days in the female reproductive system. During that time she will absorb the man's energy, so that energy, which in this case is the man and his emotional feelings toward the woman, must be healthy and positive toward her. If the semen and the intention of the man is not healthy, a strong womb will change its chemistry to kill the semen. If the uterus is without energy, it is not conscious enough to notice the danger.

In Eastern medicine, menstrual blood can be toxic to a woman if she uses a tampon and allows her vagina and uterus to reabsorb what her body is trying to expel. In terms of sexuality, the toxicity found in menstrual blood is not so dangerous for a man because his genitals are expansive and do not absorb energy.

Thus, sex can be a far more serious proposition than many of us consider, although not for moral or religious reasons. Choosing partners is based on different criteria when it is a decision made by strong Sources. Who our brains choose for us may be compatible with the logical, conscious part in charge, but our bodies have to be with the person our mind chooses for us in very intimate ways. Thus it is important that the whole of ourselves gets a vote in picking our partners. If we make a decision of that magnitude with our personal history as the only wisdom we have to draw upon, the outcome of many relationships becomes sadly predictable. Our Sources know someone's energy immediately, from a distance, and can judge perfectly whether that person is a proper partner for all of us, not just for the system in charge. When our energy is gathered in our Sources, we have far more protection than otherwise.

Habitual energetic patterns also have set weaknesses that will translate into physical and emotional vulnerabilities. In plain language, we are all stalked daily by people (unfortunately, often including ourselves) or events that can drain our energy. When our minds or expansive hearts tell us that we (as defined by that system) must always be considerate or sweet, for example, we prevent ourselves a critical level of protection. There are certain times when rage, anger or even violence is perfectly appropriate. Of course I am talking about dire situations. It is never appropriate for someone to preemptively strike someone else, unless one's life is on the line. If we disallow ourselves a true, appropriate response, we are not allowing the system designed to protect us to do its job. This is why the body often thinks we (our consciousness) want to be in dysfunctional situations; we stop our instinctual reactions until our bodies believe we no longer desire them. When we are balanced, our protective life energy has no routines, no gaps, and cannot be pierced by people, situations, viruses, etc. When we make our choices from a powerful, neutral place, we will not allow any destructive energies into our space. Those destructive energies can take the form of people, situations or emotions.

Sometimes patients speak about their most incessant thoughts. Invariably, whatever it is seems very important. It has proved useful to ask them to quantify how much life energy they are using on that subject in a percentage. That done, we would then move to the next thought or emotional attachment and quantify it. By the time we were done, they would be, to paraphrase one New Age writer, overdrawn. In other words, more than 100 percent of their life energy was going outside of themselves, leaving nothing to live on but their health.

Most of us, if we look at our energetic expenditures, are in a similar situation. We often plead helplessness about the expenditures, as if our minds, hearts or genitals are fixated on something without our permission. And yet we often treat our bodies as the whipping posts for the same obsessions. As long as systems other than our Sources have our life energy, that helplessness is real, as is the self-abuse.

However, we do not have to fight our minds, hearts or genitals about specific issues. The largest issue is where the energy is and if we are being fair, kind and sweet to our primary relationship, which shows up in how we speak with ourselves. We need not debate ourselves on how energy has been spent or why it is where it is. When the energy is in the most effective location, the issues shift and often disappear.

When women and men put their energy in their Source, they are at peace. They have the option to not expend care. By "not expending care," we are privy to the Source's viewpoint that says, in essence, "The subject is upsetting only from a mental or emotional viewpoint. From my position within my Source, I am under no obligation to invest my energy in that upset." That is, from an energy-filled Source, people have a far better perspective on the upset in question, whatever it is.

A new perspective simply means a new organization and understanding of life energy, which in turn leads to a different, more powerful view of what was so incessantly upsetting before. We are free to feel and think however we like, so long as our actions are directed by the Source's viewpoint, where everything wins.

If anything in our lives becomes dualistic, we know that we are not putting our energy in the place where we can be our full selves.

REPAIRING DAMAGE

To repair our damage from lost energy, it is necessary only to gather all our intent, will and consciousness into our Source. I say "only" as if it is simple, but this is a monumental task for most of us.

Personally, I find that I can practice only a small percentage of what I know, although that amount varies daily. Like any extraordinarily close relationship, my ability to connect to my body is changeable; we have good days and days where I distract myself completely with the external world. Finding my Source is not difficult, but I often indulge in focusing on historic obsessions because internal peace is new and still feels strange. Sometimes I can catch myself (my brain) early and offer myself new, fairer options. When I am able to do so, my life is smooth and calm. When I am okay, I feel that my consciousness is with my Source, and my primary duty in that place is to find out what I authentically define as joy for and within myself. When I find that joy, every life in my garden shares the benefit.

When I am not able to find my connection to the deepest aspect of myself, when I stay away from my Source, I find myself in a situation different from my patients in only one respect: I know that suffering is an option that I've learned to choose by default, and it is my job to guide myself to a fuller paradigm. In those moments I need to treat myself with tenderness until I've found my way back to consciousness of my self-love, back to my Source.

When we feel lost, we can start small, realizing first when we are not in our Source. Only when we start to recognize where we are organizing our perceptions from, can we start to have any choice in the matter. Where we come from now is habit. It is not necessarily ineffective, but it is probably effective at a cost to other systems.

Anything that we think about frequently and with feeling, anything that makes us strongly emotional or that we obsess about is something to which we are engaging our energy in a frantic way, which is draining. In order to cut down on that leakage, again, first just notice it. Where does your energy congregate? Where do you feel or see your life energy dull? Where is it heavy? Where is it painful? Where do you get symptoms? All these are good questions to ask of ourselves in order to become more consciously involved with what actually happens within our own walls. In this way we are attending to our primary relationship.

Our problems, issues and symptoms are the easiest clues to track the inner pathways of our life energy. Once we can recognize where our energy is and what flavor it has, we can play around with moving it easily from place to place. Once we can sense energetic movement within ourselves, many of our areas of leakage heal on their own. It is also interesting to learn which sensations translate to what thoughts. For example, when your body feels a heaviness, what does your brain tell you your problem of the moment is?

One man had an interesting experience with the above exercise. Every so often he would crave sex maniacally. He would seek pornography, he would pester his girlfriend, he would stare at women on the street. When asked to notice the next time he had an "attack," what exactly he was feeling in his body, it took him a couple of weeks to track it down. When he did, he reported that whenever he felt strong anxiety or strong anger, the "attack" hit him. When asked where he experienced the anxiety or anger in his body, he said that his anxiety was experienced as a sort of pressure in his head, and his anger was a tightness in his liver and an empty sensation in his heart.

The suggestion that came out of treatment was that he ought to sit with the feeling rather than its directives. Each time he was checking out a woman in the street or badgering his girlfriend or looking at that movie, he was just throwing his life energy out there, hoping for something to calm him. Depletion left him more anxious, which just fueled the cycle.

Clinically, there can be no judgments about what he was doing. We all do what our habitual survival measures call for. However, when objectively looking at his life energy, it seemed fairly common: He had some blocked areas that created tension. He had learned to dissipate and soothe that tension by throwing energy away. He had also learned to translate that physical tension into a physical need.

In his past, when he did indulge in sex, it only dampened those feelings briefly. Usually they would surge again quickly. His body was letting him know it had too much energy in certain places and not enough in others. His brain's prescription was sex. The fact that it did not work for more than a little while did not stop him from feeling it and acting it out again and again.

It was only after noticing where his energy was and what his brain told him he needed to do about it that he began to understand that what he thought he wanted might not be accurate. Or rather, it was accurate insofar as his habit and his brain having all the energy was concerned. It was inaccurate from the viewpoint of finding out what he wanted from the position of his Source, his heart.

To direct our energy anywhere effectively and with integrity, we must focus it through the lens of our Source. Only then are we in harmony with life.

CHAPTER FIVE

FINDING OUR HOLES AND OUR LINES

One exercise useful for both men and women is finding our holes and locating our lines. Holes are areas in our bodies that are empty of energy, while lines are what we use to catch and send energy from and to the outside world.

Thinking of lines can be confusing, but we have been throwing and fastening energetic lines all our lives. Some are severed; others are strong. Some are attached to things we would agree with if the attachment were conscious, and others may attach to things we no longer agree with. Certain lines were, when we were children, critical to our survival. As adults, lines can leave us open to being depleted, or they can be avenues through which we draw energy from others. Once we cast a line, energy can flow both ways through it. When people act from their Source, the holes heal and the lines wither. Creating a habit of existing from our Source can take time. This exercise will facilitate that process.

After a lifetime of unconscious lines, we are depleted. This depletion, either over time or as a result of a shock, causes us to develop holes. Holes are areas in our bodies or our energy fields where life energy is depleted. There is a related area where our life energy is blocked or stuck. The blockages usually result from an attempt on our body's part to cut off energy to the place where it is being depleted. In general, depletions must be fed and filled before tackling blockages. This is because the blockages will often release spontaneously once the hole is healed. If the blockage is released before the hole is healed, there is the risk of more energy leaking from the hole.

We can locate these holes in various ways. If we are visually oriented, we can close our eyes and scan our bodies for dark patches or dead areas. Sometimes an entire side will be riddled with holes or will be dark. Usually, with some focus, one can narrow it down to the biggest hole or the darkest place. Somatic people will "feel" an area that is deadened or empty. Auditory types can often "hear" where they are depleted, either verbally or through a change in their internal "sound." Usually, though, it is only necessary to close one's eyes and sit quietly, feeling the inner body. A place will seem empty or "sad" or weak.

When we have located our holes, we try to find out where the energy that was there has gone to. Some holes are created by blockages elsewhere, just as a dam creates dryness below it where there was none before. Some holes are created by emotional wounding and others by physical or lifestyle wounding. Regardless of how they were created, they must be regenerated. The purpose in finding where the energy has gone is to insure that the regenerated energy does not follow the same path. Where the energy has gone can be tracked using lines. Again, close your eyes and sit quietly, and if you focus on the hole, eventually you will receive some clarity on where its line goes to. It has proved helpful for many people to know about the cause of the depletion, but it is not critical for healing unless the person is still being depleted by the same or a similar cause.

Clinically, it is relatively easy for many professionals to determine a course of treatment that will restore an injured area. This book is mostly for people to work on healing within themselves.

For women, try to gather as much energy as you can into your womb and then ask the Source to help fill and heal the hole. If that is too vague or you need something to occupy your mind, you can visualize (or feel or hear, depending on your orientation) turquoise veins of energy flowing or snaking into the hole and slowly filling it. If the color is disagreeable, choose your own. Turquoise works well on about 95 percent of patients. This technique also works well for blockages, as they are often dark, congealed areas of energy that let nothing pass. Blue veins of light working their way into blockages is a powerful image.

For men, try to gather the energy in the heart and then ask the heart to help fill and heal the deficiencies. Turquoise can again be used for most patients who want a visual path.

After the holes are filled, you can go to work on the blockages in the same way, asking this time for the Source to help disperse the blockage.

The basic goal is to have all areas available to our senses. That is, if we are visual, we ought to be able to visualize any part of our bodies without difficulty. We ought to be able to move energy, even with visual imagination, through all the areas in our bodies without the vision fuzzing or fading or diffusing. The same is true for those with somatic or auditory orientation.

Lines are related to holes in that they often stem from them and attach to another person, event or traumatic time. There is no linear time within the body's experience; when we recall an ancient event with enough focus, our body relives it with a physiological response.

Lines are often ways we gain or lose energy. If we have had a love affair that ended badly and we still hate that person, we have a line to them and are still sending and taking energy from them. The relationship is never truly over until we have attended to our lines. If we have had a love affair that ended while things were still good and there is still a daily thought about it, there is a line to that person still, and we take energy from it. When longing for a person or situation, we lose energy.

Parents of grown children who still spend a lot of energy worrying about their relationship to them have lines from which they either give energy or take energy from them, or both. When we remember a trauma and cannot get over it or when we obsess about something, we have a line to that thing and we are sending it our life energy.

Some lines are cast from the Source, others from the remaining Heats. Source lines do not concern us, as they are not designed to take more than they give. However, the other lines can be damaging.

There are some patients who say they do not mind sending life energy to certain people they love and who need them. This is especially true for parents. What often needs reframing is the belief around love and need. When these patients are asked to define love, many interesting answers emerge. Children may indeed need our "lines" at times to keep them safe in today's world. A line thrown out when a child is in need is something few parents would begrudge. But do children need it when they are grown? Does having a fixed line really serve both or either parties? After all, energy flows both ways. If we think about what we would want as someone's child, it would often be for our lives to be our own. We may want help if we ask for it, but would we want a line or a cord of need connecting us to our parents? Do we want their energy or want them borrowing a bit of ours at their whim? This is energetic codependence.

If we want to help our grown children, we must give them respect and assume that they are whole and do not need our help unless they actually ask for it. The imbalanced connection often serves the parent more than the child because it is also a way to be needed. When parents can let go of their role at the appropriate time, the child has no onus to take care of the parent, and thus, paradoxically, is more likely to desire to do so.

In relatively equal relationships, lines can be rather innocuous. However, whatever is unknown and is leaving or coming into our bodies is a definite concern. Would it be better to know that a line was there and decide to keep it, or to have lines that extend to who knows what?

Lines that attach to people or things we hate are like pumps that take away our life energy. This depletion leaves us weak and makes us likely to go into survival mode. Going into survival mode means that we feel at risk and thus retreat to a defensive position, usually the brain, and then a triggering of our adrenals follows. Many of us are addicted to adrenaline, whether we get it from fear, exercise or coffee, and even though its overuse depletes us, we seek it again and again.

For example, the brain might buy into a definition of love or caring that demands a line to a child because the parent defines the child as helpless. That line may pump life energy out of the parent through memories or obsessions or fear, and that depletion triggers more fear, and then the brain is stuck: it obsesses, trying to figure out why the fear is there, yet it is a mistaken definition that caused all the depletion in the first place. Then the parent must psychically take energy from the child to feel better, usually in the form of demanding reassurance or the child's compliance to the parent's (fear-driven) requests. However, it is an exchange without permission and invariably ends up being depleting to the child and the parent both.

Even when we act from habit and incomplete personae, our Source is there. When we enact a win-lose paradigm, the Source will not act, and we are deprived of the wisdom of creation.

If we come from our Source, which needs nothing, these lines slowly close and wither. Our holes slowly fill. Then we can give and receive from a place of fullness, and there is no emotional or mental charge around it.

We ought to have no lines to anybody or anything, unless they are cast or accepted by our Sources. Our small children certainly do not need unclearly cast lines. They model themselves on us; if they see us energetically use lines in dysfunctional ways, they are more likely to do so.

Small children are capable of seeing energy on a broader spectrum than we allow ourselves to admit, until they are taught what not to see by watching us. It is far-fetched to believe that a child can see emotion, feel logic, and hear colors. Far-fetched, but possible. Who can quantify what children are capable of perceiving before they are socialized? How can a child explain what they experience if we, their elders, have no language for it? If our children see us whole and contained and coming from our Source, they can mimic that and spare themselves and our world any more of this stress and confusion.

CHAPTER SIX

EXERCISES

We all organize our personae and identities around different places in our bodies. The less fluid our identities are, the fewer options we have, the less life energy we can express, and the more likely we are to become either stuck or overwhelmed. Eventually this lack of fluidity begins to limit our body and its movement. Only when we have an abundance of life energy stored within our Source can we access any and all of our qualities at any moment and be flexible. When we come from our strong Source, we are always appropriate to our own sense of what is right. We need nothing and so are not vulnerable, except as we choose to be.

A brief note: While some of the following exercises may be of interest to the younger reader, it is my recommendation that boys and girls wait to try them until the onset of puberty. That is, when men start to ejaculate semen (or reach the age of sixteen) and when women start to menstruate. Some women do not menstruate owing to various factors and so if a young woman has not reached menarche by the age of fourteen, she may try the exercises in this book. The reason behind this limitation is merely that the energetic configuration of children is different from that of adults. Children's energies are not mature until they organically achieve the ability to reproduce, and thus ought be allowed to do so undisturbed. If, however, at any point anything becomes physically uncomfortable (and this goes for all readers), please stop and seek appropriate help.

There are those who may experience a kind of backlash from the exercises and the premise presented in this book, but this backlash is mostly a return to a habitual pattern of emotional or logical experience, and as such is not dangerous. It is ultimately worth noticing, even if it proves annoying. Backlash is something that can occur whenever the body is asked to experience anything new. Putting our energies down different paths almost invariably produces survival reactions.

There are several ways to determine the place from where we usually organize our identities. The first, and perhaps easiest, is the following:

DETERMINING OUR PLACES OF PERCEPTION

FIRST POSITION

- *Lie on your back in a comfortable position, where you will not be disturbed.*
- *Close your eyes.*
- *Inhale through your nose and breathe out through your mouth.*
- *Inhale and exhale again, longer, through your mouth.*
- *Repeat that breath cycle one more time.*
- *Ask yourself what percentage of life energy is in your brain.*
- *Note it, and then ask yourself what percentage of life energy is in your heart.*
- *If you are a woman, ask yourself what percentage of life energy is in your Source (womb).*

- *If you are a man, ask yourself what percentage is in your prostate or genitals.*

  Women can also ask how much life energy is in their genitals.
- *Note the percentages. If they total more than 100 percent, rearrange the numbers until you have an idea of the approximate breakdown.*
- *If under 90 percent, please locate the unaccounted life energy.*
- *Inhale through your nose and exhale once through the mouth, and open your eyes.*

Of course, these percentages will be fluid. Always pay specific attention to the first answer you are conscious of. When we are stressed, there is more energy in certain places and less in others. However, this ought to give a fair idea of which Heat you are organizing your identities from. Try the above exercise when you are feeling good and then when you are feeling bad. Try it in the morning and the evening. After using the exercise lying down a few times, see if you can do it sitting up and merely closing your eyes. Then see if you can tell how much of your life energy is in your Three Heaters just by concentrating. The objective of this exercise is to increase your awareness of who you are and how you feel when your energy is in specific areas and at certain amounts.

Some patients report seeing a number when they ask what percentage is there. Others report getting a sense of weight, and still others report just knowing how much is there. We are, of course, talking of conscious life energy. There is, as mentioned previously, subconscious life energy and unconscious life energy. Later, when we perform exercises to shift the balances of life energy, it is useful to remember that we are playing around with only our consciousness—not with anything that will stop our hearts or brains from living or even functioning perfectly well at an organic level.

It is common for female patients to have 60 percent of their life energy in their brains, 30 percent in their hearts, and 10 percent in their wombs.

Men often have 60 percent in their brains, 10 percent in their hearts, and 30 percent in their genitals.

See what your specific percentages are. This can tell you what percentages of life energy create specific personae within our consciousnesses.

It is interesting to note that a large number of people, especially menopausal women, have an energetic organization in the physical location of the solar plexus. If you are someone who has a lot of tightness there or digestive difficulties, check what amount of energy is there. If you become aware of any other areas in which there is discomfort or pressure, determine the percentage there as well.

The next step after discovering how our energy is distributed, is communication and negotiation. We must, as clearly as possible, learn to distinguish between the internal communications of the hemispheres of our brains, our hearts, our wombs if we have them, and our genitals. For most of us, once we get our minds around the concept of "giving voice" to various parts or heaters in our bodies, it is remarkably easy. Thespians are usually adept at this immediately, but others require practice.

Query the part in question, and pay attention to the immediate reply that comes to mind, even if it is obscene or if the part is silent. All communication, even the absence of it, is useful. It is helpful, for example, to know if your mind refuses to even talk to you about shifting life energy.

Simply put, the mind is logical, and things must be safe and make sense. The heart feels emotion, and the genitals are occupied with thoughts or feelings about sexuality, sensuality or physical satisfaction. Sometimes the heart or brain is so involved in genital energy that we can confuse sexuality with an intellectual component or with love. The quality of the sexual thoughts can be either preoccupation or denial. It can take quite a lot of sexual energy to repress sexual energy.

In some of us, internal communication is vague. Still, we all have moods which are an excellent window into the tenor of our internal communication. Our emotional tenor, as well as its physical location or heater, is a constant companion that communicates our internal weather deftly once we develop the willingness and ability to look for it.

Once we have some idea of the differences between heaters, we begin the negotiation. We first ask the brain what percentage of energy it is willing to reduce to. At first we will ask to try this new balance for half an hour. The brain needs two to four percent of conscious life energy to function well. If the brain balks, we explain that it is an experiment and that the brain can pull the energy back if it needs to. Try to get your brain to agree to reduce to five percent. After all, it is only for half an hour. An analogy that often works for the brain is as follows: Ask the mind if it has ever lived or spent time in a big city. Ask if it was easier to drive around at 2:00 a.m. or during rush hour? In every city I've ever lived in, the answer is 2:00 a.m. Then ask the mind if it is conceivable that less energy can allow things to flow easier.

Then, if you are a woman, ask the heart and genitals to also agree to reduce to five percent. If you are a man, do the same thing for the genitals. In short, do it for any place that is not the Source. By the time you are done, try to have permission to play around with 80 to 90 percent of your life energy. Permission is critical, since the Source will not take energy unless it is offered. The one exception is with most women during pregnancy, when the Source usually takes the energy needed and the woman and the pregnancy are the better for it.

Once permission is granted, lie down and repeat the First Position's initial breathing sequence, and then move into the Second Position if you are a woman or the Third Position if you are a man. Note that the opening breathing sequence for the Second and Third Positions is opposite from that of the First Position. It is useful to read the position through first, so you can do it with your eyes closed. Remember to take your time. If at any point you lose the ability to shift energy, return to the First Position and find out where the largest percentage is being held. That will be the area blocking further exploration, and that is the system that needs more communication and negotiation.

SECOND POSITION

- *Inhale through your mouth and exhale through your nose three times.*

- *Ask your womb to gather the energy the other systems have liberated.*

- *Fill your Source with 10 percent of your life energy. Give yourself plenty of time.*

- *When the Source has gathered the energy, check with yourself. Does your womb feel different? If so, how? Notice it.*

- *Gather again, going up to 20 percent life energy in your Source.*

- *Take your time. How does that feel? Is there any difference?*

- *Slowly continue to gather energy into your Source in increments of 10 percent.*

- *Pay attention to how you feel as the energy becomes fuller in your womb. If at any point there is resistance or the movement is sluggish, ask your womb again to help draw energy down.*

- *When the percentage is more than 50 percent, note how that feels.*

- *At 60 percent and higher, see if your brain feels different, and see if your heart does as well.*

- *At 70 percent and higher, you ought to be able to get a good sense of what the Source feels like.*

- *After it is as full as you will allow, just lie with it and notice again how it feels. How does your brain feel? Your heart? Your genitals? Your stomach? Scan yourself entirely. Then see if your other systems, feeling as they do now, will allow the womb to have any more energy.*

- *Once all the energy you have available is collected within the Source, it is time to open your eyes.*
- *See how much life energy immediately shifts upward. Notice it, and try to let the womb re-collect it.*
- *Next try moving. Notice and re-collect.*
- *Next, reenter your life.*
- *Notice and re-collect whenever you remember to.*

THIRD POSITION

- *Inhale through your mouth and exhale through your nose three times.*

- *Ask your Source (heart) to take the energy the other systems have liberated.*

- *Fill your Source, your entire chest, with 10 percent of your life energy. Give yourself plenty of time if necessary.*

- *When the energy is in the heart, check with yourself. Does your Source feel any different?*

- *If so, how? Notice it.*

- *Next, gather 20 percent of life energy in the heart and thorax. Take your time.*

- *How does it feel? Is there any difference?*

- *Slowly continue to collect energy into the Source in increments of 10 percent.*

- *After each increase, see if any sensation within your body has changed. How do you feel as your chest becomes full?*

- *If you feel the heart is becoming congested, then feel your ribs open out, or open in, or somehow slide to the side so that there is plenty of room.*

- *Allow your heart to slowly fill. Each 10 percent ought to create some change, however slight, in the feeling of the mind, heart and genitals.*

- *When you reach the place where the heart will not take any more in, see if your brain or genitals are blocking it. If so, renegotiate.*

- *If not, ask your heart to help draw the "free" energies into itself.*

- *When you have reached your limit, take a moment to notice how your brain feels.*
- *Is it quiet and dark or otherwise? How does your heart feel? And your genitals?*
- *Then open your eyes. See if the percentage shifts. If so, re-gather the life energy into the heart and chest.*
- *Next try moving. Notice any changes and collect any possible energy into your Source.*
- *Then enter your day.*
- *Periodically try to notice where the energy is and re-collect it as necessary.*

These positions are useful in introducing yourself to at least two things. The first is that our feelings change as the concentration and location of our life energy changes. The second is that at least some of our feelings or thoughts are under conscious control in the form of shifting life energy.

In the Second and Third Positions, use whatever method feels easiest. Visualizing and feeling the shifting of energies are the most popular methods. Do not be concerned if you fall asleep or if your mind wanders. That is often our mind's way of stopping something that scares it. Just repeat the position when you can. Many women report that there are one or two "walls" or "veils" that they reach, that at certain percentages it becomes as if the uterus will not take in any more—but it will. The womb can expand to take in 100 percent of your life energy and more. After the "wall" is reached and passed, it gets easier. Take your time. It may take quite some practice to experience even 70 percent life energy in the Source.

For women who have had hysterectomies, try to feel your energy pool in your pelvic girdle. That, energetically, is the cradle of a woman's Source. In

Eastern medicine, the organ is just the most physical manifestation of the systemic energy.

An effective visualization for women is to imagine the energy being liberated from the heart or brain congealing into a ball of turquoise light. This ball drops from the organ down onto the spine and rolls down along the spine. When the ball reaches the coccyx, it rolls up into the womb and is absorbed.

Men should use the spine as a track that guides the energy either up from the genitals or down from the brain to the heart and chest.

For women, the next step is most easily explained to women who have given birth. Most mothers have a strong recollection of how it felt to have a baby inside their womb. The feeling of a full Source is similar to being pregnant, without any weight. After a woman gets her mind around the possibility of feeling "pregnant" without being pregnant, she ought to be able to grasp the following concept: Just as she carried a life inside her womb, so can her womb carry her, as its creation, as its "child." Many patients have reported that there really is no difference for the womb to nurture a life inside itself or to nurture the woman it is inside of. The Source simply nurtures. Thus we have a paradigm shift, and when this shift is made, the power of Creation that exists within the womb becomes as the parent, and the woman who has the womb becomes as the child. She is protected, as her children were protected, by the field generated by the energy-filled womb, and protected by Creation itself.

For men the next step is more vague. We have no system that is concretely connected to internal creation. We do, however, have a connection to protection energy and the energy of movement. A woman's energetic configuration is based on Earth energies, and a man's on heaven or sky energy. As such, men's energies are more changeable and more diffuse.

When we have gathered all our energy into our hearts and opened up to receive life energy from the world, the next step is to allow our heart energy to course through us, blowing like a wind, opening all our blockages and dead areas. We can use the metaphor of thunder to shake loose deadened areas or blockages. We allow our full heart energy to sweep us clean, leaving us like an untroubled blue sky. By definition, men (not boys—boys and girls both need a tremendous amount of nurturing) require less nurturing than women, and women require less movement and protection than do men.

Both sexes, when in conscious contact with the Source, are at peace. The Source provides fulfillment, stillness, movement, protection and anything else the moment needs. By trusting the energy that brought every one of us into the world, we are cared for. When we seek our genesis in this way, men and women can be whole within their own skins. When two whole people come together, it is out of choice and not from seeking something external to complement our dominant personae.

The path to "God," mystery or Spirit for women is through their energy-full Source. There is no external power for a woman. For men, our path to the same qualities is through our full, open Source interpreting the external world.

Yang energy (men) needs the external world. Yin energy (women) may want elements of it, but does not need it. The outside world is the only field in which yang energy is capable of giving birth. It gives birth to ideas, businesses, refinement, art, etc., in the field of the perceived world.

I would like to introduce two additional exercises for returning life energy to the Source. The first exercise is called Source Inspiration. It is quite quick and simple. The second exercise is called the Inner House. It uses metaphor, the language of our inner world, to connect more deeply with our bodies. The warning that accompanies the first exercise is self-explanatory: as this is a breathing exercise, please do not practice it while doing anything else that requires your undivided attention. This exercise can cause some dizziness. It is not, for example, recommended for use while driving. However, some patients have reported doing it successfully while waiting at long traffic lights.

SOURCE INSPIRATION

- *Three times, in your head or aloud, repeat the word Intent.*
- *Mentally or verbally state your intention to have all your life energy be liberated and go into your Source.*
- *Take as long an exhale as you can, and then inhale as deeply as you are able to.*
- *Hold the inhalation, the inspiration, trying to feel the energy going to your Source.*
- *Hold your breath as long as you comfortably can, and then release it.*
- *Return to normal breathing.*
- *You may repeat this exercise up to three times before taking at least a five-minute break.*

THE INNER HOUSE

The second exercise, the Inner House, uses a metaphor that seems to help people strengthen the links between their inner and outer worlds. It is based on a simple, ancient idea: Our body is our temple. To remove it from religion, think about your body being your house. If the idea that your body houses your spirit, consciousness or soul makes sense to you, this exercise should prove interesting. If you have trouble visualizing, just say the first thing that comes to mind. There is no right answer, so do not worry about what comes up.

This can be difficult to do alone, but it has proved to be a powerful visualization. Although most patients have been delighted with some of the discoveries they have made with this exercise, a few have experienced some fear and surprise at what they have found within. While I believe that a single person can easily go through the necessary steps to make this exercise effective, some people may want to have another (trusted) person present to act as a guide, using the outline provided.

Five percent of patients experience a physiological reaction during this exercise. If you experience an unpleasant physical reaction, washing your face and arms with cold water should calm things almost instantly. I have not seen evidence of any harm stemming from this exercise. However, I have a healthy respect for the large variety of responses people can have when stumbling across things that scare or confuse them. When one patient first visualized a certain room, she was shocked at how empty and dark it seemed. She began to hyperventilate until I instructed her to make windows. Within 10 seconds she was breathing normally again. Some people visualize their Inner House with such intensity that it is felt externally.

THE EXERCISE

Please repeat the opening breath sequence from the Second or Third Positions.

If your body is your house and a house is comprised of rooms, then ask yourself this question: If my brain had a room, what would it look like? Would it be big or small? If you know what it would look like, then describe it. Is it an attic? Is it a computer room? Is it an office? One European woman said that her brain room was the kitchen. In her family, everyone did his or her work in the kitchen, on a long counter. What room is it for you? How big is the room? Is it neat or messy? Does it have windows? If so, are they large or small? Do they look out over a pleasant scene or a stressful one? Are there other people in this room? If so, how do they respond to you and what are they doing?

In short, picture this room as completely as you can and then imagine walking into it. What is the first thing you feel? Is it positive or negative or a mixture of the two?

Once you have a feeling about the room and have noted it, you are hereby given unlimited power and funds over the room. Renovate and redecorate. Make it larger, if you wish; allow the windows to look out over the landscape of your desire. If something strikes your fancy, do it. Change the room to what you would have in your best, wildest dreams. The only rule is that, as this is your house, you must inhabit it alone, at least initially. There can be, and probably will be, rooms you invite people into, but to start, they must not be an intrinsic part of your Inner House. They have their own houses. Pets, spirits, plants, etc. are fine.

Some people find that certain inner rooms are behind closed doors or are locked or cannot be found. If the door is closed, open it. If it is locked, see yourself with the key or cause the door to fade. If the door refuses to open or the key cannot be found, create the room anyway; bypass the unavailable room. If the room cannot be found at all, create it fresh.

Once you envision the perfect brain room, see yourself walking in again. What is the feeling now? If there is the merest hint of a negative feeling, ask yourself what element you could add or subtract to neutralize that feeling? What needs to be changed or taken out? Plants, skylights, fountains, music, views, a change in the room's shape or color are all ways the room's mood can be improved. If you have pictures on the walls, they can be of people or things that encourage and inspire. Anything that has a mixed emotion attached to it can be changed or let go. Since this is your room and your body, you can even change the expression of the people in the pictures.

One man had a picture of his father in one of his rooms. He felt many conflicting emotions having that picture there because he had many conflicting feelings about his father. Yet he definitely wanted it there. I suggested that he picture his father smiling at him, and when he did, the conflict of emotions was gone. He just felt good about it.

You are the deity in your inner world. Please do not stint on pleasure.

As a general rule, the brain's room seems to require order. Many people also find that a comfortable place in the room in which to relax makes the brain room even more inviting.

Next we descend to the heart room. This is the room of a man's Source and the room that houses a woman's emotional life. Patients typically see it as the living room, the bedroom, or, sometimes, the library. Again, picture it completely. Note the size of the space, the windows if any, the colors, the furniture, the floor and ceilings. If there are windows, how big are they and what views do they have? Picture yourself walking in. What emotion comes to you? Does the room feel congested or empty? Does it feel relaxing and safe, or is there a stressful feeling that comes to you? Does it make you feel sad and lonely or full and happy? Once you know how your heart's room feels, go on to redecorate and renovate. As this is a man's Source room, men should make it an amazing place that they never want to leave. Some rooms in people are already perfect for them. Many need to be changed, to be enlarged and enlivened and made more comfortable and beautiful. If you fall into the latter category, enlarge it, put in a fireplace or French doors that go out onto a patio, or a deck overlooking a beach.

One woman's heart room was completely Moroccan in style. It was red with pillows everywhere, music was always playing, with wine and grapes and huge windows that overlooked the sea.

One man's Source room was a huge living room with very little in it. It had a vaulted ceiling and windows that looked out into forest, a large chair that he sat in, and his long-dead childhood dog next to the chair. Another man said he loved his heart room: It looked like his living room at home. The only problem, he said, was that the temperature varied wildly: it was always too hot or too cold. I had him picture his favorite sitting place and put, within easy reach, a thermostat that always worked. After that, he decided to also add a fountain and a courtyard with a fish pond. Those additions helped him feel serene and in control of the climate.

Another woman read Architectural Digest to find elements for her inner rooms.

Continue to visit and improve your heart room until there are only positive feelings when you enter.

Moving down the body, we come to the Stomach, and if it was not the brain room or the heart room, picture it as your inner kitchen. See it fully. Is it a lovely place from which to nourish yourself? Is it cramped or spacious? Can you enter it easily? Is it dark or bright? Clean or messy? Does it have the elements needed to relax you and your loved ones? Does it open onto a herb garden? Does the view from the windows, if any, please you? See it completely and then imagine yourself entering it. How does it feel to you? Renovate and redecorate. Get the finest appliances, if you like that. Have it open and spacious and airy, or small and intimate. Whatever you desire. Make it perfect for yourself. When you have changed or created everything that occurs to you, imagine entering it again. How does it feel this time? Add things, remove or change things until the feeling is as good as you can get it.

We then move farther down the body to the intestines and bladder—the inner bathroom. If the bathroom was, by some chance, one of the aforementioned rooms, then it is already remodeled. If it is not, follow the principles outlined above: What does it look like initially? Make the picture as clear as possible, then enter it and capture the present feeling.

A patient with irritable bowel syndrome found her inner bathroom door locked. She knocked the door down (she was rather impatient to see this room). She said it was a perfect, spacious bathroom, but it looked as though it had never been used. The feeling she received when entering was one of relief.

Renovate and redecorate, as if money is no object (internally, it is not). Then reenter the room and assess the feeling again. Change, add or eliminate things from the room until it feels perfect. Common additions to the bathroom are: more space, big tubs, a deck, thick towels and bathrobes, plants, music and skylights. Some have outdoor bathrooms. A majority of my patients seem to prefer open-air beach views.

As we continue to move down the body, this next room is for women only. What does the womb room look like? See it completely. Is it comfortable? Does it have or need windows? What feeling do you get when you enter it? Does it feel as comfortable, safe, and relaxing as it can? What needs to be added, expanded, or changed? Does the color of the walls suit you? Whatever it takes to make this room a beautiful, peaceful destination, do it. As this is the most important room in a woman's body, make it a spectacular space you wish to stay in. Reenter and see how you feel. Continue to play with it until the feeling entering this room is perfect.

Women may desire to see themselves nursing a baby in this room. It is fine, of course, to see your child or children within this space with you.

Then we move to the last of the rooms found on the center line of the body, the genital room. In this room, repeat the instructions just presented. I have found that while a great many men and some women make this the bedroom, many also make it outdoors. When I asked one woman how she saw this room initially, she said it was like a prison cell. It was small, bare, and gray, with high, barred windows. Her feeling on entering the room was cold, sterile, impersonal and imprisoned. She was laughing when she described it because she said the visual was a complete surprise but explained a lot. She ended up throwing that whole room away and starting over.

Make sure your genital room is comfortable, lovely and safe. Make it a place you can relax in and enjoy.

One man wanted his wife in this room. He said that since she was the only woman he could ever see himself with, he wanted her there. But the only way he felt peaceful with that was if, in this room, she was always open, playful and available to him.

As it was his body and his room, I did not say anything. I thought that perhaps when she was not open, he would not invite her into this room. Later, they divorced. From my view, his genital room (root attitudes and sensuality toward yin and women) was wrecked for quite a while. It seems to make more sense to make this a room for self-fulfillment, exploration and safety.

So, if you must place a partner within this room, make sure that your partner's attitudes contribute to your sense of peace, fulfillment and fun.

I have said that I generally discourage people from placing people in the inner rooms. Although it makes sense to me to have places in some rooms for people to visit, we ought to use caution about the people we actually make part of our rooms. Of course, the final decision as to whether or not you place people in any of your rooms is and must be yours alone. You can always change the room if it does not feel right. However, my strong suggestion is that we make no energy intrinsic to our inner rooms but our own.

Once you have finished the genital room, go back through your Inner House and see each room again. See if the feelings remain constantly positive, and change the things, if any, that need it. Once all your rooms are perfectly at home for yourself, ask yourself if you need any other rooms.

For example, one man I treated was a martial artist. I suggested that he might want a room in his liver, which in Oriental medicine is responsible for martial energy, to place his. His liver room turned out to be a combination armory, meditation room, library and sparring room.

Perhaps singers need a room for the vocal part of themselves, athletes a field, and actors a stage. There is a whole world within us. Create any rooms you require, adhering to the same principles detailed above.

Once you have your Inner House, there is one more part. It will take time, but it will be enjoyable. Its purpose is to create a link between the inner and outer worlds.

Find one item from each of your inner rooms. If you do not already have it, track it down in the external world and place it in your external, everyday world house. Whenever you see that item, it will create a link to your inner room.

Symptoms also have rooms, and it is a powerful healing exercise to determine what those rooms look like and what elements within them contribute to the feelings that are inherent in the symptoms. What is felt when the room is changed? And can the original positive intention of the symptom be included in a different, more effective way?

For example, one time when I was very angry I took a moment and pictured the room in which my anger lived. It was small, irritatingly hot, with a hissing voice telling me what other people wanted and how I was lacking. There was also a huge clock that always indicated that I was fifteen minutes late. I changed it to a large grassy garden, with a chaise, a cool drink, and a good book. I pictured myself there, reading and sipping, and called up a cool breeze. I was astonished to notice my mood shift instantly. The underlying intent in my original room was that I would never be late or lacking in my service to others. I decided that the original purpose was no longer pertinent, because I no longer wish to be beholden to anyone external for my actions or promptness. I realized that to my Source, my service to others and being prompt was a matter of my own personal pride. Reliability had become a part of my character that I could trust and rely on without the need to drive myself to those qualities with internal pressure. This room exercise can be done with headaches, depression or any other identifiable symptom.

How many spaces within us languish merely because we were never taught to look inward in a pragmatic, reassuring, sweet way? How much of our life energy is stuck in pointless loops or ugly rooms when changing them is so easy? We can give ourselves permission to love our Source as the primary relationship in each of our lives and see how well our gardens bloom.

One reason this exercise is so powerful is that it is easy for most people. I've had many conversations with patients about ease. The outer world paradigm is that anything worth having has to be worked at, suffered for, and is difficult to attain. That is often true in the outer world. However, in the inner world everything wants our experiences and growth to be fluid, joyful, neutral and easy. If we superimpose our external paradigm on our inner world, we will be moving at a constrained speed that creates symptoms. If we realize that internally, peace can be as omnipresent as air and that it ought to be effortless, we can have another inkling of how our Sources want our lives to be. Our Sources believe we should have peace, love, joy and fulfillment simply because we are. Do our minds and hearts agree?

In terms of the Inner House, we have made our rooms beautiful. If all rooms are lovely, then wherever we find ourselves internally will strengthen or relax us. Once we find, for example, our Source room, we can go there instantaneously. Instead of having to meditate on dropping percentages, we just picture ourselves entering our Source room, and once we've learned to trust ourselves, our consciousness will go there, along with all its energy. If there is work to be done, we can enter our brain room. When we are relaxing with friends, we can go to the living room, or we can go to the kitchen when nourishment is of the essence.

Another reason why this exercise is effective is its ability to metaphorically create a room out of a configuration of life energy. Anything we do, feel or know can be said to have a specific form of energy. When we feel a familiar symptom, emotion or state of being, we are metaphorically in a specific place, which can be visualized, felt or heard as a "room."

I have found that I can go to my Source room and stay there, often without thinking about it, because it is the room in which I feel strongest. It becomes the place where I am when I am not thinking about it.

This exercise can be combined with the Source Inspiration by holding the breath at the same time as visualizing the inner room. The more real and detailed the visualization of the room, the more energy is there.

The Inner House exercise takes the shifting of energy away from the need of convincing the brain or heart (for women) that they should let energy go. This can be difficult because the dominant persona, besides being attached to its power, is also attached to its dysfunctions, addictions, symptoms, and neuroses.

With the Inner Rooms exercise, we simply visualize a room and the energy inherent in consciousness comes with us.

For some people with kinesthetic or auditory organization, this exercise may not be effective. They will still need to negotiate with the expansive systems. I offer it because it seems prudent to know how to do both — to deal with the expansive systems consciously and also to bypass them by using an internal metaphor.

It would be nice if we never had to fight or experience conflict. By that I mean externally, but I also mean avoiding conflict within our own brains, hearts and genitals. However, conflicts happen, and it makes sense that we have the means with which to face them. With practice we can develop the skills and the insight needed in order to differentiate between the energy that attacks and that which is besieged, as well as the energy that is always fine. Of course, the aspect that attacks us is also us, but it is a part that has identified itself as different, sometimes superior, to the whole. The errant part must be recognized as us, even if it is using an attitude or a viewpoint learned from others, be it familial, religious, racial or societal.

It is also my hope that at some level, the errant parts that disown us are taking this information in as well. At some moment in this lifelong relationship to self that we are all engaged in, knowing or not, we must own all our parts with all their various desires and opinions. At the same time, to ever be at peace and in integrity, the disowned parts must also own us. Whether we approach this through metaphor or negotiation, it must be done.

Within the Inner House we are all the rooms. Our consciousness merely visits one or the other. The metaphor can bypass conflict by taking the movement of energy out of the framework of winning or losing, or of giving or taking. All our rooms coexist right now. The questions are, which rooms do we spend all of our time and consciousness in? Which rooms feel the best at any given moment, and which bring peace to the entire Inner House? So, if all our rooms are created to our specifications and we have conscious choice, which room will we spend more time in?

From our Sources, which are our peaceful, beautiful, safe homes within, we will be able to participate in all of our relationships, be they internal or external, from a more relaxed and powerful place.

I hope that the previous chapters will give the reader other options for ways to communicate with one's various parts, or heaters, just as the Inner House exercise will give the reader options in the movement of energy.

CHAPTER SEVEN

DROPPING AND CONTAINING

The Second and Third Positions both have to do with dropping and containing the Life Energy into our Source. We have all been taught or have learned to keep our energy in a certain configuration and density through experience and habit. The new positions have to be experienced in a safe way because shifting our life energy means leaving the known and entering the unknown, which often triggers a measure of survival. The only reason it is possible for anyone reading this to pursue the movement of energy is only because it is not leaving our body. We are not giving it away; rather we are moving it around within our selves, and thus we can reason with our various systems to just try it.

As our systems experience the lessening of stress and tension, they are more likely to return to the Source just because they have never before experienced a conscious pathway to peace. It is seductive to be able to identify a part of ourselves that is always fine and go there at will, because this is what we are all looking for in one way or another.

We are ineffectively taught to seek comfort through interacting with the external, yet the state of being fine is an internal matter. We have learned to interact with the world through expansion, yet balanced interaction stems from a receptive place. When balanced well, humans take in a phenomenon, digest it, and then react. Reacting from systems that are not designed to keep the whole of who we are in mind makes us shadows of our human potential.

We men are taught to initiate movement largely from our upper or lower heats, where it is in the middle heat that a man's Source is found.

It has long been modeled or forced upon women that they must expand their energy and personae from the upper or middle heats, or from the genitals acting as colony for those heats. Women are most powerful in the lower heat. Both sexes have learned to act from where we are the least capable of holding power. It is a simple maneuver, once we know this, to seek the most effective, balanced way to organize ourselves.

By dropping not only our life energy, but also by letting go of our habitual defense of the status quo, we allow ourselves to feel what actually works. Our brains can come up with argument after argument, but they will all dwindle when the mind finally has a chance to relax and shed the mantle of ruler—a position that has been foisted on it, a position that the brain took because is was taught that it had to.

The ability to feel at peace is the first casualty, the first conscious awareness of loss of harmony, of yang acting without yin. Only yin can direct yang from a joyful, neutral, relaxed place. Millennia ago, the most successful races (if we define success as the ability to exact bounty or tribute from one's surroundings) were the ones that moved violently away from yin being honored for first, and into yang taking whatever it could overpower or outrun. We have, slowly and steadily, moved away from any paradigms our ancestors knew to be true wisdom, and more toward survival.

A definition of magic, according to Webster's, is any mysterious power or phenomenon that defies analysis or explanation. To me, the entire inner life is magic. Synaptic function, the miracle of breath, experiencing love, anger, openness, anything really, has the potential to be magic if we are focusing our attention on the part of us that is living magic, the Source.

Power is seductive only if you care. It is a temptation or a burden if we put power in a place designed to care (yang needs to care in order to protect). Dropping our life energy from the mind to the heart and raising it up from the genitals to the heart is the first step for men. The second step is learning to contain it there, to make it the receptacle in which life energy rests, without having to think about it. In other words, to create a habit of putting our energy there.

For women, it is simpler. Women just have to drop and drop and drop further. Eventually it all comes down into the womb. And after the energy descends into the womb, it is a matter of repeating that sinking down until it becomes a habit and energy moves there without thought.

CHECKING OUT

"Checking out" is vernacular most of us are familiar with. It often happens when a system is being asked to let go of its energy and then, in the midst of the exchange, gets scared. Many patients will start to drop energy, get scared, and then either start talking about something that brings energy to the system in fear, drift off to sleep, or report more energy in their Source than is actually there. Patients may report 100 percent life energy in their Sources, yet it is evident to a trained observer that they have shifted less than half of that. Some will say that they simply cannot move the energy any further, while others will use a symptom to distract themselves.

If, during practicing the Second or Third Position, you find your mind wandering and no changes in your sensations within the three heaters, see if you are somehow checking out. There is no need to force anything and, indeed, no way to do so, since the Source will never resort to acting against

Itself. Checking out tells us that a system has gone into some level of survival. At that point, the fear has to be identified, even if it is simply fear of the unknown, and it must be put to rest, if possible. Again, if you are unable to calm your own fears, it may be necessary to seek help.

RESPECT

Respect is the most necessary part of any practice. We must respect our desire for peace, but we must also respect the parts of us that fear it. We must respect the systems that are not designed to rule but think they have to. They have identities that are not to be crushed by any autocratic or dualistic thinking. We must respect that we will have resistance, which is just as much part of us as the parts that desire freedom. We must respect our speed of change and our speed of letting go of ineffective habits. Pushing too hard can slow us down tremendously. Often just an intent is enough. An intent, stated or thought of enough, will slowly begin to guide us to those experiences.

We must respect that we are mostly lost, but can be found. Respect that we are trying hard to grow, but also trying hard to stay with what might be uncomfortable but is known. Respect that survival wants to keep us living but has no idea how to help us feel alive. Respect that survival might even want to see us dead rather than unsafe, which being alive might be. Respect that the experiences that led to such a brutal system of mind were in fact filled with fear and hurt and cannot be merely thrown out. Respect that the only time survival can actually relax and our wounds can actually heal is when our energies are within the Source. Respect that we are beings filled with contradictory thoughts, feelings and desires. Respect that we want to change and that we do not want to change. In short, we must respect who and how we have been before we can guide our energy into the totality of who we are. So if our minds, hearts or genitals balk at change, shirk at letting energy go to the Source, be patient. Experiment and experience as much as you can, but do not force it. Respect your timing, and respect that you may not know what your best timing is.

Intent is one of the most subtle and powerful forces in the universe. Use it. Respect that it is a force and as such has its own wisdom, timing and intelligence.

CHAPTER EIGHT

TOOLS AND MODALITIES

There are many paths to help us effect a change in our options about how we organize energies within our fields. The main internal tools that seem effective are as follows.

1. Respect the timing our Sources have. As mentioned, once we want something, we must respect the path our lives travel to get there. For some, even knowing that we have a Source is enough. We are not taught that within us is a kind, capable, patient Source that will guide us whenever we give it the power—which is life energy or consciousness—to do so. Once we know it is there, it is merely a matter of time before we get to it.

2. Intent. If we, every morning when we wake up and each evening before we sleep, simply state our intention to have all our energy stored in our Source, it will get there. Intent is all we need, but it needs to be a consistent focus. We need to continually redirect our attention toward the Source in order to create a habit of organizing from there. Intentions are the easiest ways to know what we desire to see happen.

3. Patience. It takes time to create new habits. It takes time to get the parts of our bodies that are accustomed to having so much energy to recalibrate themselves to their original designs. It takes time to learn to trust parts of ourselves that seem foreign. It also takes patience to allow who we are to slowly manifest onto the stage of the world. We will be different when guided differently. We will drop certain connections and forge new ones. At a slow speed, all these changes can happen organically.

These three tools are useful because they are inherent in the Source's viewpoint. The Source contains all these qualities and more. If we find ourselves acting or thinking without respect, intent and patience, we are not within our Source. It is sometimes easier to tell where we are not than to know where we are.

4. Humor. The more humor a person sees in life, the easier it is to shift life energy. Also, the Source is not all that serious. Nothing external is very serious to the Source. The most serious Sources often get is describing worry about their person, i.e., the personality that is running things. Self-importance is a sign of being stuck outside of the Source's field, and humor saps self-importance.

The next tools offer more specific ways in which we can actively do something to further our connection to the Source. Intent was included above because it is something you do and keep always in the background. While the first four tools deal primarily with our attitudes, the next tools are to be practiced whenever possible.

5. Nature. When we spend enough time alone in nature, our speed automatically begins to slow. Since our Source is by definition Nature, any time spent in natural surroundings will help us put energy where it is most effective. If nature is to be used as a tool, it is important to spend the time in nature not doing anything "productive." Sitting, walking slowly, especially off the paths, looking and breathing, are all recommended to use nature as a tool to return to our Source. It is sometimes inexplicably more powerful to travel in nature with nothing that is metal. The theory is that metal on a person interferes with the natural world and its communication with us.

6. Silence. Trying to exist without our internal continuous dialogue is an excellent practice. To achieve even 10 seconds without a thought, observation or comment is very difficult. Our Source maintains silence unless asked. Silence will help us access the subtleties in our inner landscape more effectively. Communication without the brain's input is primarily through sensation in women and emotions in men.

7. Unusual Activity. When we do things we do not usually do, we enter the unknown. It takes us out of habitual response

and invites us, especially if we are conscious, to organize ourselves in a new way. It gives us opportunity to develop our persona around the energy of the Source. Some examples of unusual activity include walking backward, taking different routes—especially routes that are longer that may have only beauty to recommend them—shaking our bodies without rhythm, being actively silly, dropping water balloons on friends (if this is unusual), drinking or eating something completely different, not defending something, defending something, reverse blinking, etc.

8. Beauty. Seeking out whatever is beautiful to us is another good way to jolt our habits into doing something new. Just the act of trying to be in the presence of beauty will show self love.

9. Omens. Whenever you note something unusual, try to also note what you are thinking about in the moment or feeling or doing. See if whatever was unusual has a message, even if that message seems strange. For example, when dwelling on some problem and then seeing an animal, note what kind it was. Was it a skunk? A dog or a cat? What do these animals mean to you on a visceral level, and what were your thoughts just as you saw it? It takes time to learn to accurately read what omens mean, but as there are probably a hundred a day if we are looking for them, there is time to learn.

10. Beliefs. Set a timer to go off randomly. Whenever it goes off, write down what time it is, what you are doing, and what you are thinking. After doing this for a week, write down after each entry if you agree with the belief behind the thought and which heater you were acting from. Some patients report that there are certain blocks of time where nothing they are doing or thinking is congruent with their Source and other times or activities that are exactly congruent. When blocks of time ruled by the mind, heart (for women), or genitals are discovered, we can apply the seventh tool, Unusual Activity, to them.

11. Prayer Or Meditation. This aspect of communication with Spirit is not particular to any religion. It is a means of gathering one's energy and then opening to something larger than the self. In my view, the Source is our internal manifestation of Spirit, and so, by communing with the Source, we are communing with Spirit. However, this internal connection has a different feel from an external one. Whether we contact the Source externally and that contact reflects internally, or we keep the connection internal, is unimportant. The only importance is that we connect with Spirit (the Source) in some way. It is essential that the contact be experienced as benevolent.

12. Loyalty: This is one of the most important issues in this book. So much of our suffering and depletion comes about because of unexamined loyalty. Most of us have had years

while growing up where we witnessed things that did not work harmoniously. Yet those we loved repeated those dysfunctional acts again and again. Our loyalty might cause us repeat the paradigm merely because we loved them and this was how we witnessed them act. We have the option as adults of taking any issue and seeing if it stems out of loyalty. What do we think? If we feel and act in the ways that cause us stress, does it remind us of anyone? A mother or father, perhaps, or a grandparent? Or a teacher or a religious or political belief? Examine it. If it does not make your life and the lives of those you love more beautiful and peaceful, see if you agree with it. After all, we as adults can continue to love whomsoever we chose, but we are not compelled by that love to act as they do or did.

For myself, I refuse loyalty to anything that does not embellish my life and the lives of those I love, and I will be loyal to things that cause all parties to prosper.

Search through your own loyalties, and drop the ones that cause pain and depletion. Drop the ones that make you feel bad. By being loyal to our own Source, we and our children will have a chance to choose how we experience life. We owe loyalty to our primary relationship with ourselves. If we treat ourselves poorly and say things internally that we would not say to a loved one or to a stranger, we are not being fair. To avoid hypocrisy, we must speak and act toward ourselves as kindly as we do to anyone else we know or might meet. This, of course, is assuming that we know how to be kind. However, almost everyone is kind to at least one person, animal or plant in the world, so they know how to be sweet in at least one instance. It is a matter of treating ourselves with the best we can muster.

There are many other tools. Meditation is useful for slowing down and getting out of the mind. Having tea with a friend can also provide calm, which in turn makes it easier to give energy to the Source. Anything that makes us happy is a tool. Whatever we feel an obligation to do, or what we think will be good for us or others, is likely not helpful. That which we have to push ourselves to do, or that which we have to do, is not a useful tool for this way of approaching life energy. The Source does not push, force, judge, need, or guilt us into doing anything. The Source never says "should," or "must," or "have to." Application of those qualities and statements will not lead us back to them.

Different modalities of treatment are useful in giving our bodies and brains more options. Below are a few specific recommendations culled from my own and my patients' experiences. In general, if you see someone whose life energy you respect, ask him what he is doing. If a person is capable of putting 90 to 100 percent of life energy into her Source, healing will be largely spontaneous.

For the body, any modalities that change the way we feel or offer us new areas of ourselves to explore are useful. Acupressure, moxabustion, acupuncture in experienced hands, Chinese herbs, Feldencrais, Alexander Technique, Rubenfield Synergy, craniosacral, Acutonics, shiatsu, skilled massage, or any of a plethora of old and new treatments can trigger new experiences and help us unblock our physical body. We must seek out physical treatments that resonate with our own understanding and feelings.

Our bodies will usually know immediately if something moves us. As with any therapeutic experience, we must be able to trust the practitioner's integrity and skill. Avoid shocks that weaken the body unless the need for them is well explained and their duration is made clear.

For the mind, Eye Movement Desensitization and Reprocessing (EMDR), Neuro-linguistic Programming (NLP), and visualizations are all powerful for certain people.

Of course, there are thousands of practitioners of numerous modalities doing wonderful work. It is often a matter of playing the numbers until you find the person who can help you get to your next step. There are often therapists, both physical and mental, who will help guide you toward a goal. Those therapists can be helpful if you state your goal as getting to your Source. Therapists who focus on where they think you should go, on what they believe your "problems" are, will not be useful unless you agree with them from your Source, not your logic or sentiment.

Whenever we go to a therapist or a doctor, it is vital that we use them as our Source uses our other parts, as a means to help us experience and realize our intentions. We are not there to make them right, to rehash our old stories, or to stay in an imbalanced function within ourselves. A good therapist is there to help us become more at home in our own skins. A good doctor is there to present us with a neutral view of our condition; a great doctor or therapist will care only that you flourish, whatever that looks like for you specifically, and then direct you to other options and opinions to help you do that. In short, all helpers should aid you in getting to where you want to go in the most clear, beautiful way possible. It should never be about them.

The effort to reach our Sources is the path to the true awareness of being alive. Once we reach a place where we can store our life energy in our Sources, we will have arrived at a place of true healing. We will all experience it for ourselves.

In closing, I would like to thank the hundreds of patients who have supported my inquiry with their patronage, friendship and trust. Thank you to the teachers, writers and to nature for being a steady source of inspiration and fortitude. Thank you to my dad and sisters for being behind me. And most especially, thanks to my family, my son and his mother, who have shown me what it means to be alive.

Of course, my deepest gratitude and love always goes to my mother, who brought me in and guided me to this path.

Dr. Imetai M. M. Henderson completed his two-year basic course in acupuncture and Oriental medicine at the Kototama Institute, Santa Fe, New Mexico, in 1985. At 19, he was one of the youngest Americans to be Board Certified and State Licensed to practice acupuncture in the United States. Subsequently, he attended a two-year internship in Santa Fe, followed by a three-year internship in New York City. From 1989 until 1993, he participated in an externship under the guidance of O'Sensei M. M. Nakazono, the founder of Inochi Life Medicine and of the Kototama Institute. Dr. Henderson has also studied the Japanese martial art of aikido since the age of four. He presently holds the rank of Yondan (4th Degree Black Belt).

Dr. Henderson has been in private practice in New Mexico, Connecticut, New York, and Colorado for more than 20 years. In 1995, he developed Source Medicine and founded the Red Branch School of Oriental Medicine. His school respects the traditional teacher/apprentice paradigm, and the ancient medical connection to Budo.

Source Medicine combines the traditional forms of acupressure, acupuncture, moxibustion and diet, along with spiritual and emotional insights, as directed by traditional Five Element Diagnosis and Treatment.

You can e-mail Dr. Henderson at: imetai7@gmail.com.